The Holy Women
Around Jesus

Other Books by Carol Haenni, Ph.D.

Anna: Woman of Miracles

The Holy Women Around Jesus

Carol Haenni, Ph.D.

ARE
PRESS

**ASSOCIATION FOR
RESEARCH AND
ENLIGHTENMENT**

A.R.E. Press • Virginia Beach • Virginia

A.R.E. Press
215 67th Street
Virginia Beach, VA 23451-2061

Library of Congress Cataloguing-in-Publication Data
Haenni, Carol, 1932–
    The holy women around Jesus / by Carol Haenni.
        p.   cm.
    ISBN 0-87604-509-3 (trade pbk.)
    1. Women in the Bible–Miscellanea. 2. Jesus Christ–Friends and asso-
ciates–Miscellanea. 3. Bible, N.T. Gospels–Criticism, interpretation, etc.–
Miscellanea. 4. Cayce, Edgar, 1877-1945. Edgar Cayce readings. 5.
Emmerich, Anna Katharina, 1774-1824. Leben unseres Herrn und
Heilandes Jesu Christi. I. Title.
    BS2445.H34 2006
    232.9–dc22

2006013156

Cover design by Catherine Merchand

Contents

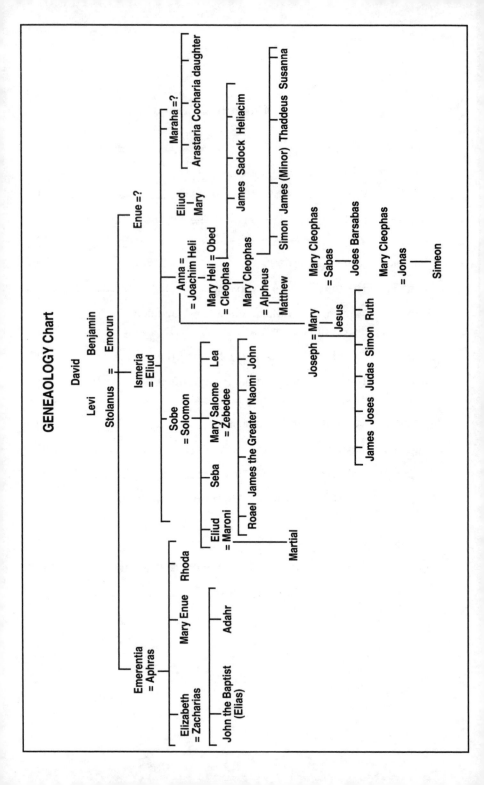

GENEAOLOGY Chart

Introduction

*I*n this book the veil covering the hidden holy women, living during the time just prior to, during, and after the physical life of Jesus, will fall away and reveal a group of diverse, dedicated women, who, greatly inspired by Mary, the Blessed Virgin Mother, serve God and Jesus, who becomes the Christ. Since there is scant information about these women in the Scriptures, two main sources give information that breathes life and individuality into these special women. In his readings for certain individuals, Edgar Cayce describes past lives, usually giving the person's name for each lifetime. The focus is on those designated as holy women living during Jesus' physical presence on earth. The German nun, Anne Catherine Emmerich, presents these women in such rich detail as they traverse her vast world of visions that we feel we are there on the scene.

Edgar Cayce, at times, while in the trance state, converses with people on the other side. Emmerich, at times, interacts with beings in her visions. In order to help the reader better comprehend how both Cayce and Emmerich experience their readings and visions—as though there are no boundaries of time and space—as much as possible, the book is written in the present tense.

Who are these two people? Edgar Cayce was born on March 18, 1877, in Kentucky and died January 3, 1945, in Virginia. He was called a seer, prophet, and mystic. His psychic readings, given while he was unconscious in a self-induced trance, number more than 14,000, are well documented, and are available on the Internet.

Anne Catherine Emmerich, born in Westphalia, Germany, on September 8, 1774, died in Dulmen, Germany, on February 9, 1824. She, like Cayce, was born on a farm and received a limited formal education. She worked on the farm, then became a servant girl and later a seamstress. At the age of twenty-eight, she became a nun for ten years. She was exhibiting the stigmata even before entering the Augustinian convent. After Joseph Boneparte suppressed religious communities in 1811, Emmerich spent her remaining years, ill and bedridden, sheltered and supported by townspeople. She suffered greatly from the effects of the stigmata and especially from severe headaches associated with the crown of thorns.

After his first visit to the nun, Clemmons Brentano, a well-known poet and literary figure of the time, abandoned his career and spent the rest of his life recording and organizing her visions. Presently, the Roman Catholic Church has elevated Emmerich to the beatification level, the last step before the designation of sainthood.

For the sake of brevity and minimum interruption of the text, relevant source identifications appear in the text. Information from the Cayce readings is referenced by the number assigned to the person receiving the reading and, after a hyphen, the number of the reading being given for that person. Material from Emmerich's visions is referenced by the initials ACE in parentheses followed by the relevant volume of the four books and the page number in that volume. My resource for the Emmerich visions was the four-volume set, *The Life of Our Lord and Saviour Jesus Christ,* but the reader may find them available on the Internet and in other collections, though the pagination may differ. Any other sources are named in the text.

Chapter 1

Who Are the Holy Women?

*I*t is not possible to give an exact list of the women who can be designated "holy women." Both the Cayce and Emmerich sources lack a
definite list of criteria for applying the label. There seems to be a general grouping and then a more specific grouping within each source. In
each case, the holy woman designation tends to refer to special women
from an earlier time. As a group develops, the criteria within the readings tend to become more specific (but never clearly stated). In each
instance, the Virgin Mary is the nucleus of the group. The purpose is to
provide first a channel for Jesus and then to be a support group for Him
and His mission, creating a general boundary for the holy woman label.

It is important to remember that those called the holy women are
not officially part of a group given that name but are called by that
name well after the fact. The term "holy woman" may raise varied
thoughts in people's minds. A generic concept of a woman particularly
devout, spiritual, and giving may possibly be a common description
awakened in the minds of those hearing the term, "holy woman." This is
a good foundational image for the group as a whole. However, there is
no official list of characteristics and requirements that a woman must

1

meet to be declared a holy woman, nor is there any official list of names.

Many of the women in the Emmerich visions and the Cayce readings remain nameless, and some women are named but not designated holy women. In some cases a woman may be declared *not* one of the holy women (with no explanation).

Gladys Davis, Edgar Cayce's secretary, addresses the fact that a person is often called by various names (1152-3). The options include surnames, nicknames, Hebraic or Arabic names, and in Emmerich's case Germanic names. Because people often share the same name, confusion may occur as to which Mary, Salome, Susanna, etc. is the specific person in question.

It is helpful to become acquainted with some of the statements made about holy women and their responsibilities by the two main sources, Emmerich and Cayce. First, there are those associated with the desire to provide a channel through which the Messiah may come into the world and fulfill the promises and prophecies of the Hebrew Scriptures. The Essenes (meaning expectancy, according to Cayce) are a group very much dedicated to this mission. There is no mention of the Essenes in the Old or New Testaments, but both the nun and the prophet designate the Essenes as those most attuned to the fulfillment of the ministry of Jesus (in contrast to a great many of the Pharisees, Sadducees, and Herodians). As a whole, none of the groups understand that the Kingdom of God, as Jesus teaches and illustrates it, is not of this world. Because those in high positions in the Hebrew religion do not comprehend, they feel threatened by the teachings of Jesus. Therefore, they often do not cooperate with Him, and, finally, seek to rid themselves of Him because they fear He wants to usurp their authority, and crown Himself king.

There is no exact starting point for identifying the holy women in the Cayce readings. One reason for this is the method by which he obtains most of his information. Much to Cayce's surprise the concept of reincarnation appears in readings; so he begins to give past-life readings. A person might receive a reading that mentions a past life in which the term holy woman appears. Then, Cayce may give another reading for more information about the past life in which this title holy woman appears. Some receiving readings learn they were once one of the young girls chosen to prepare to be a possible channel for the Messiah. Mary is one of the twelve young girls. The purpose of bringing these girls to the temple is to prepare them to consecrate their lives and prepare their bodies and minds to be of service. All go through rigorous training of body, mind, and soul so that one from the group may become the channel for the Messiah. The training prepares all of them to be of service in some way or other. We will soon take a closer look at those in the group obtaining readings from Cayce.

At this point a greatly condensed sketch of events that lead up to the time of Mary and Jesus helps give a basis of understanding for subsequent events and persons involved in them. The cause and effect sequence appears more clearly in the visions of Emmerich because they are generally arranged in more chronological order. Edgar Cayce, while quite sensitive even as a child and quite psychic throughout his life, is often dependent upon receiving information by being given a name or being asked questions while in a trance state. After returning to his conscious state, he learns what he has said from the conductor of the reading (usually his wife Gertrude or his secretary Gladys Davis). These two sources complement each other, give us different perspectives, and certainly add greatly to the information in the Scriptures.

In Volume 1 of *The Life of Christ*, Emmerich describes the fall of the angels. After becoming obsessed with self, they are gathered around a dark disc below against their wills. Other angels take the places of these angels and seek pardon from God for the self-obsessed angels. Emmerich discerns that the strife is not to occur above but below, and that the physical world is far more beautiful before sin enters. Concurrently, Edgar Cayce states that the only sin is selfishness, and selfishness is not pretty.

Emmerich describes the creation of Adam and then the creation of Eve, taken from Adam's right side as he slumbers. She comments that, if not for the fall, all would have been born in this manner. She observes a globe of light enter into Adam's side, and calls it the threefold germ of God's blessing. She sees it withdrawn from Adam before he sins and remarks that the blessing given to Abraham is one diminished from the blessing given Adam. She perceives that the globe of light placed in Adam was to form a pure offspring. She sees a tower about which the angels work as God reveals to the angels His plan for the redemption of man.

The blessing passes on from patriarch to patriarch until Moses builds the Ark of the Covenant, takes from Joseph's body the blessing (or holy thing), puts it in the Ark, and leads his people out of Egypt carrying Joseph's remains and the Ark of the Covenant with them (ACE 1-109-117). In the middle of the Ark is a little door, nearly hidden, whereby a priest can remove the holy thing. It is possible for the high priest, with covered hands, to remove the holy substance and plunge it into water. Emmerich tells that this occurs at the time of Anna's conception as her mother Ismeria receives the holy water to drink, which is then passed into Anna. Deborah, the prophetess, and Anna, the mother of Samuel in Silo, also receive this sacred draught. Finally, it is taken from the Ark in the Holy of Holies, placed in Joachim's breast, and causes the conception of Mary when he embraces Anna in the passageway beneath the temple (ACE 1 129-145).

The nun feels there is a relationship between the holy substance of the Ark and the blood and body of Jesus in the Holy Sacrament. She bemoans the unwillingness of so many of the Jews to accept Jesus the Christ as the fruition of their desire for a savior. As for Edgar Cayce's twelve readings discussing the Ark of the Covenant, the primary conclusion is that when the Prince of Peace comes, the meeting with the Holy of Holies takes place in the heart, the mind, and the understanding of the individual, due to the New Covenant embodied in Jesus the Christ (5177-1).

Chapter 2

Defining Holy Women and Their Purposes, Duties, and Plans

*R*emember that the title "holy women" is not immediately bestowed upon women at the time of their actions but after the fact; no doubt many women involved before and after the seminal event may also be called holy women. For both Edgar Cayce and Anne Catherine Emmerich, the Virgin Mary is the central holy woman.

According to Emmerich's visions, the purposes and plans of the holy women become rather formalized at a gathering at the house of Lazarus where about sixteen men and seven women gather (ACE 2–173). After the arrival of Jesus and the serving of the meal, Jesus gives instructions. The men share experiences encountered. The women, after hearing these experiences, talk among themselves. The women include Seraphia (Veronica), Johanna Chusa, Susanna, Mary Marcus, the widow of Obed, Martha, and her old servant. Because public inns often refuse to serve food and lodging to the men, they are experiencing difficulty in meeting basic needs, so that hardships result. Private inns can change the situation, and the women will be in charge of establishing them and supplying them with whatever the traveling Apostles, disciples, and Jesus might need. Jesus accepts their plan, and it is agreed that the women are to be advised in advance as to where and when groups are traveling so that the relevant inn will be ready to receive Jesus and His followers. About fifteen inns are created—some belong to Lazarus, some to members of the holy family, and some newly created, will be scattered over the country. Districts are set up and assigned to specific women. They list the needed supplies and services and determine which person will be responsible for specific items and chores. Martha happily makes plans. The women devise a game to benefit the enactment of their project. Emmerich describes the game in detail. It involves the women's pearls and other precious stones as prizes which fall into drawers previously assigned to each woman. They institute their plans, and increasingly her visions show the disciples, Apostles, and Jesus traveling to the inns, and the holy women and permanent residents or caretakers furnishing the food, basic needs, and services.

The Twelve Maidens Prepare

Now it is time to become acquainted with individual holy women. A good place to start is with the twelve young girls chosen to train for service and, possibly, as the channel for the Messiah. In answer to a question regarding the choosing and training of these potential channels, Cayce replies that the parents dedicate the daughters and prepare them physically, mentally, and spiritually to serve in this very special way (254-109). They train vigorously with physical and mental exercises and receive extensive schooling in such character traits as being pure, chaste, loving, patient, and enduring (5749-8). They must eat properly and exclude all fermented drinks.

Anna carefully nurtures and trains Mary, so that upon presentation to the Essenes she proves to be so exceptional that they accept her. But they do not believe Anna's claim of Mary's Immaculate Conception.

Two women receive Cayce readings indicating their participation in the selection process of the twelve maidens: Shalmar (2520-1) and Anna, who he also calls a holy woman (2603-1). Shalmar, considered a sage, knows well the Essene priests of Carmel, studies the teachings of Persian, Indian, Egyptian, and Hebraic groups as well as others, and participates in choosing the twelve. Anna, an assistant to the authority figures in the temple, is influential in making the choices. Later, she sees Jesus blessed in the temple. Another Anna, well versed in astrology, numerology, and the sages' mysteries, apparently makes the final choices of the twelve based on her perception of their depth of truth—important so that the Holy Spirit may move them (2408-1).

In a reading, Edgar Cayce says about Sofa:

> Before that the entity was in the land of promise; being among those peoples who had accepted the teachings as to the manners in which there was the looking for a Messiah, a Prophet, which had been proclaimed of old.
>
> The entity was among those of the household of faith in that direction; not only embracing the Jewish activities but the Essenes' interpretations of same.
>
> Hence the entity was acquainted not only with those of the house of David through whom there came the forerunner, the prophet, but the Messiah, Jesus Himself. Thus the entity was acquainted with many of those whose children were destroyed, though none of the entity's were offered, for in the experience the entity was never wed but led the life of the celibate.
>
> And the entity counseled with the mothers of many of those who hoped for the selection of their offspring as the channel for that prophecy; also caring for many of those.
>
> Hence the entity was among those of the period who are termed in the present as the holy women; counseling with the mothers and the young during that period.
>
> The name then was Sofa. The entity gained, the entity lost, for with the activities which apparently allowed the edict of the king that brought destruction, was it not even the prophetess itself—*this* entity—who wrote that song of Rachel's weeping for her children?
>
> In that the entity brought into the minds of many disturbing forces; not intentionally, not purposely, but because of overzealousness.   2173-1

Sophie, an Essene from a family which descends from the house of David (not related to Joseph or Mary), trains with Mary and sees her chosen on the stairs by Gabriel (245-1). Although Sophie has doubts at times, she believes and is present at the cross.

Andra is another of those whose lives are dedicated to service and who train with Mary (649-1). The reading implies that she is a holy woman involved in preparing for the disciples' needs as they travel about the country. She works with specifically named persons: Zebedee's children and families, the wife and mother of Peter, and the brothers, Thomas and Luke. She receives credit for preparing the napkins placed about the head of Jesus at his burial. A son-of-David seal and a pear and bell with pomegranates on either side, possibly embroidered by Andra, appear as symbols on the napkins.

Cayce refers to one of the twelve as the other Mary (2946-2, 3). In her third reading is this statement: "We find that the entity was among those of the group selected as channels considered worthy for the incoming of the promise of God with man."

Both readings refer to Mary's close relationship with the Zebedee family, and to the holy women. She takes care of James and John in the household "that entertained the Master oft." This other Mary is especially fond of John, Apparently, John thinks highly of this "lady elect" to whom he, in their later years, directs the second Epistle of John, which consists of only one chapter.

This other Mary and John and Mother Mary become especially close after the crucifixion when John assumes the position of son as designated by Jesus from the cross. The reading refers to the two Marys as becoming "bosom friends."

Cayce credits this Mary with giving aid and inspiration to the disciples and Apostles. She had many years to interact with these followers of Jesus, since "the entity lived to be of great age."

The third reading states that the other Mary is the wife of Roael, the oldest of the children of Zebedee. At their wedding, water is turned into wine. Whether or not the other Mary is ever the wife of Roael remains to be determined. The third reading does not mention Cana.

Another reading refers to Clana as being a cousin of Mother Mary, and a daughter of Elizabeth's younger sister, also named Mary (5749-15). The reading states that Clana marries Roael in Cana (609-1). Clana's reading relates that she "was the bride for whom the first of the miracles was performed by Mary's son who became the Christ, the Lord." Perhaps the answer to the wedding puzzle involves more than one wedding taking place in Cana with Jesus turning water into wine more than once. There are certainly enough women named Mary to cause confusion.

Among those first chosen of the twelve was Edithia (587-3, 6). Her parents are of the Essene sect of Jews and work at preparing for the Messiah and the changes to be brought about in the order of things. They believe that the people of Israel are chosen by God to serve mankind. Mankind to them means men and women—not men as masters and women as servants. Rather, the person for whom they prepare will give a correct interpretation of mankind's relationship to God and the true meaning of "the seed of the woman shall bruise his head." Further, the beloved Son will enlighten mankind that the Holy of Holies is within and will provide a way to return the wayward to the Creator. The readings also state that Edithia is there at the inn where Mary gives birth, and she sees the baby Jesus, the shepherds, and the wise men. She knows "Mary, Martha, those of the household of Cleopas, those of the household of Anna, of Joseph." She hears John call Jesus the Lamb of God when John baptizes Jesus (John 1: 29-34). She is a part of the crowd crying "Hosanna! Ye come in the name of the Lord!" Edithia is with the holy women who act for the family as mourners for Mary, when Jesus is taken.

Josie, the daughter of Shem and Mephibosheth, is close to Mary when the angel selects her in the temple of the Essenes (1010-17). It is here that Judy, the head of the Essenes, interprets such experiences from Egypt as the Temple Beautiful and the Temple of Sacrifice (1472-3). After the marriage of Joseph and Mary and the birth of Jesus, Judy requires that someone accompany the holy family on their flight to Egypt and during their stay there. Herod's orders to kill the male children two and under in order to eliminate the baby of whom the wise men speak necessitate the flight. The White Brotherhood selects Josie to care for

Mary and Jesus on the trip and during the stay near Alexandria. Josie and Mary study in the library there and report findings to the Brotherhood in the Judean country. When the family returns to Capernaum after about four and one-half years, Josie remains with the family and helps with Jesus' education, household duties, and the other children of the Mother Mary as they are born. Josie goes with the family to Jerusalem when Jesus is twelve and stays at the temple. Mary thinks Jesus is with Josie on the way home. When Joseph dies, Josie closes the eyes and helps with the burial. She is the one who informs Mary of Jesus' arrest and urges her to go to Jerusalem. Josie never marries and is among the holy women. At the burial of Jesus, Josie brings the spice and ointments. Following the beheading of James and the subsequent riots, Josie dies.

Two other members of the twelve appear in the Cayce readings but are not named. The one identified in 1479-1 is an Essene of the household of a kinsman of Joseph, the husband of Mary. The kinsman is also named Joseph and is of the line of David. This entity loses a son to Herod's destruction of the innocents and is greatly distressed. She works with the holy women and gains from the sacrifices and later persecutions. Also, in her later years, she is one of the first to realize the freedom that women gain due to the fact that Jesus comes into the world through Mary, the Holy Virgin.

The third maiden on the stairs when Mary is chosen appears in Cayce reading 1981-1, which gives no name. She becomes the wife of James, John's brother. It is James who converts many Romans, and his wife becomes well acquainted with the wife of Cornelius. This member of the twelve walks to Emmaus with the disciples. She is among the holy women who help with Jesus' burial preparations. She is with the disciples and Mother Mary at the empty tomb. It is her husband James who is beheaded and becomes the first of the Apostles martyred.

Mary, the chosen channel, is leading the twelve maidens as they go up the temple steps to the altar in the Essene temple in Carmel (5749–8). The early morning sun shines on these steps for the first prayers, and incense burns before the altar. This particular day sunlight fills the area, casting purple and gold everywhere.

Just as Mary reaches the top step, the angel Gabriel appears to the accompaniment of thunder and lightning. Gabriel takes Mary, who is between twelve and thirteen, by the hand and leads her to the altar. In this manner she becomes the one chosen to be the channel for the Messiah.

Anna, Mary Heli, and Mary Cleophas

We know that Ismeria and Eliud have three daughters: Sobe, Anna, and Maraha. Sobe is eighteen years older than Anna, and Maraha is at least five years younger or as much as eleven years younger than Anna (ACE 1 123-4). After naming Anna the future mistress of the household and telling her she must marry, Ismeria falls sick and dies. Anna is about seventeen at this time. By divine direction Anna marries Joachim, and Mary Heli, the first daughter, arrives. She is not the special daughter anticipated. Nineteen years later Mary, the Blessed Virgin, arrives. By this time Mary Heli, married to Cleophas, has a daughter, Mary Cleophas, who is quite little when Mary the Virgin arrives, and she plays with baby Mary (ACE 1 154-5). However, before Anna gives birth to Mary, she asks Joachim to send for three women to come to be with her at the time of Mary's birth. The three women include Maraha, Anna's sister who lives at Sephoris, the widow Enue, a sister of Elizabeth from the Valley of Zabulon, and Mary Salome, Sobe's daughter and the wife of Zebedee (ACE 1 149-153). The women arrive, and Anna tells them that the germ given to Abraham by God is ripe within her—a clear reference to the holy thing taken from the Ark. The women gather and sing a psalm which includes God having pity on His people by freeing Israel and fulfilling His promise to Adam that the serpent's head will be crushed by the seed of a woman.

Anna is filled with light, and a vision of Jacob's ladder appears to the women. The women take rest, but Anna remains praying. She later awakens the women and asks them to pray with her. From a little closet in the wall she takes a box filled with sacred treasures, such as a bit of Sarah's hair, some of Joseph's bones, and a cup of Abraham's associated with the Blessing he received. The Blessing is described as an invigorating, supernatural food, a sacrament like bread and wine. A great light fills the room like the burning bush and surrounds Anna in such a way that Emmerich is unable to see the flame move inward. The shining Mary appears in Anna's arms. The holy women bathe and wrap Mary. They and Joachim take turns holding her. Then they place Mary beside her resting mother. The nun sees the reaction to Mary's birth in limbo. Patriarchs are joyous. Adam and Eve joyously recognize the fulfillment of the promise made to them. Nature rejoices; birds sing. However, possessed beings make horrible sounds that arouse Simeon in the temple. He goes to the possessed and asks the cause of their shrieks. An evil spirit replies that a virgin is born, and he must vacate the being he possesses.

The next morning a crowd gathers, and the women show Mary to them. Mary Heli is not present at the birth as it is against Jewish custom for a daughter to be with her mother while she gives birth, but she is there in the morning. Little Mary Cleophas strokes baby Mary.

Although Mary Heli could not be present at her sister's birth, she is present at the feast in Anna's house for the ceremony to name Mary. Anna's younger sister, Maraha, Elizabeth's sister Enue, and many of Joachim's relatives are also present at the ceremony. Anna does not appear but stays in her room behind the fireplace. The priests are in front of the altar. Enue brings the baby Mary, wrapped in red and white, and Joachim takes Mary and puts her in the head priest's arms. The priest holds her up, prays, and then puts her in a cradle on the altar (ACE 1 153–6). The priest cuts bits of hair from the middle and both sides of the baby's head and burns the hair in a pan of coals. He then anoints Mary's five senses, using his thumb to press ointment on the heart, mouth, nose, eyes, and ears. After this he writes "Mary" on a piece of parchment which he then lays on Mary's chest. The women sing songs.

Emmerich mentions that Anna and her third husband have a son but gives no name and indicates he is often referred to as Jesus' brother. She says that due to the abundance of grace bestowed on Anna at the conception of Mary, it requires being consumed, and thus the additional marriages and children.

Cleophas is Mary Heli's first husband, and Mary Cleophas, who is a few years older than the Blessed Mary is their daughter. Obed is Mary Heli's second husband. In addition to being the nephew of Anna the Prophetess's husband, he is a server in the temple, and a relative of Seraphia (Veronica), a holy woman. He receives baptism from John, is present at Jesus' baptism, and is a secret follower of Jesus (ACE 1 397, 405, 422, 443). The three sons of Mary Heli and Obed are James, Sadoch, and Heliacim (ACE 1 3-5). These half brothers of Mary Cleophas are much younger than their half-sister and closer to the age of her children. These sons are disciples of John the Baptist. James is as old as Andrew. Later, after Jesus' death, he becomes a priest and a very distinguished and elderly disciple. Mary Heli's grandson, James the lesser, son of Mary Cleophas and her first husband Alpheus, a widower and father of Matthew, becomes Bishop of Jerusalem.

Years later when Jesus walks with Eliud, a very enlightened elderly Essenian, they converse about many things. Eliud asks why Jesus didn't come sooner to the earth. Jesus replies that he had to be born to a woman in the manner that all would have been born if it had not been for the fall. At last, the ancestral line of Anna and Joachim and the couple themselves are pure. His birth is possible (ACE 1 1368). Jesus further remarks that Anna is more chaste than any woman ever and the fact that she twice married after Joachim's death is in accord with God's plan that this branch produce the destined number of fruits.

Emmerich discusses Anna's other two marriages and offspring in her vision of Jesus' birth to Mary. Anna comes to visit Mary, Joseph, and the baby Jesus in the cave with her servant and second husband, Eliud. She brings many gifts to Mary and the baby even though she previously sends much by way of servants. Since Mary and Joseph know the Wise Men are coming, Anna goes to spend eight days with her younger sister, Maraha, located about three hours from Bethlehem. Maraha lives in a former house of her parents. Maraha and her husband have two sons, Arastaria and Cocharis—both of whom later become disciples (ACE 1 360).

The holy family is in their house in Nazareth. Anna and Mary Heli and her child are there, too. All are sleeping. A shining youth appears at the side of Joseph's bed, speaks to him, and takes him by the hand to fully awaken him. The angel disappears. Joseph knocks on the door of Mary's compartment and goes in to talk with her. Next he goes to the stable for the donkey and begins to prepare traveling needs. Mary quickly arises and dresses for travel. She awakens Anna, her mother, and Mary Heli, her sister. The mother embraces her daughter over and over. The sister weeps and weeps. Baby Jesus is taken from His bed when all is ready for the flight. All press the baby Jesus to their hearts. It is close to midnight when Mary, holding Jesus, seats herself on the animal's cross-seat, and they start toward Anna's house. At the cross-road there are more embraces before the holy family heads away. Anna and her daughter and grandson head back to the house. Mary Heli goes to her mother's house to send Eliud, her stepfather, and a servant to Nazareth where Anna is packing up the belongings to be taken to her house. Then Mary Heli and her son go to her home.

Again and again Mary Heli appears to Emmerich as one of the holy women tending to the inns. When Mary Heli is nearly seventy, she lives in Japha, about an hour from Nazareth. She and her second husband Obed bring with them a donkey loaded with presents for Mary.

On another occasion, when Jesus goes to Nazareth at the urging of some Pharisees, He visits His parents' house. Mary Cleophas looks after the empty house and keeps it in good repair. Jesus visits his aunt Mary Heli (ACE 3 133-7). He does not stay with His relatives but with the family of Jonadab, one of His disciples. The Pharisees fault Him for this and for much else, too, but Jesus makes the statement that only in a prophet's home town is the prophet without honor. Another irritation for the Pharisees is Jesus' telling His disciples that He is sending them as lambs before wolves, and that those who refuse to receive them are going to be more condemned than Sodom and Gomorrah. Further, He is not there to bring peace but a sword.

About seventeen women, including Mary the Mother, and John the Beloved follow Jesus as he carries the cross to Golgotha (ACE 4 265, 267, 330-42). Mary Heli is one of the group. When they reach the place of execution, they see the cross, hammers, ropes, and huge nails, but Jesus they drag into a nearby cave while the executioners prepare everything. Mary Heli is in the second group of holy women standing back a bit from the first group but closer than the third group. In John 19:25 Mary Heli is one of the four women standing by the cross. As soldiers remove the body of Jesus from the cross, Mary Heli sits in silence on the wall of earth and observes the proceedings. She is an elderly matron by now. While Nicodemus, Joseph of Arimathea, Abenadab, and John carry the body of Jesus on a leather litter, Mary the Mother and her elder sister are the first two following it. After the burial, Mary Heli, John Mark's mother, and some other women take Mother Mary to the home of Mary Marcus.

Mary Cleophas is just a little girl at Mary's birth and plays with Mary, her aunt. Mary is between three and four when she has her presentation at the temple. She has a delicate body structure, is quite tall, and has golden hair that curls at the ends. She is ready to make the commitment to enter the temple. After the priests thoroughly examine her, they lead her to her mother.

Anna hugs and kisses her, but Joachim, deeply affected, simply takes Mary's hand in a reverent manner. Mary Cleophas happily hugs her aunt as a child would do (ACE 1–156, 162). Emmerich presents her vision of the procession to the temple with Anna, Mary Heli, and Mary Cleophas leading the way. Mary and the other little maidens follow, all dressed in special dresses, decked with garlands and carrying candlesticks. They take a round–about way and pass by the house of Seraphia (Veronica), who is probably twelve at the time. Emmerich has Mary going to the temple in Jerusalem whereas Cayce sets the place of training at the Essene temple in Carmel. Whether Mary spends times at both places is not known (ACE 1 162, 171). It is obvious that Mary Cleophas and her Aunt Mary are quite fond of each other and work together as relatives, holy women, and fully committed helpers of Jesus.

Through Emmerich we learn that Mary Cleophas' first husband, Alpheus is a widower with a son Matthew, a publican. Mary Cleophas does not like that occupation and grieves over Matthew, but Jesus, who knows Matthew and his potential, comforts His cousin by telling her that Matthew will one day be a fine disciple. There is not much information given about Mary Cleophas and Alpheus having a daughter, but that is not really surprising as the Bible mentions few women, and the whole culture at that time gives men prominence and women, for the most part, insignificance. At a time when Jesus is speaking to many people in Peter's house, we learn about Susanna in passing (ACE 3 73–4, 125). Mary the Mother arrives escorted by a group of women: Martha, Dina, Susanna of Jerusalem, and the daughter of Mary Cleophas, Susanna Alpheus, who is about thirty and has Apostles as brothers. Her husband lives in Nazareth where she joins the holy women. She has grown children. The account also notes that Susanna Cleophas desires to serve Jesus and the disciples and be admitted to the Community. Whether this is another name for Susanna Alpheus or a different Susanna will be determined later. The sons of Mary Cleophas by Alpheus are Simon, James the Less, and Thaddeus. Simon is a clerk or magistrate, while the other two are fishermen. Joses Barsabas, also at the fishery is a son by Sabas, Mary Cleophas' second husband. In time, Joses becomes the first bishop of Eleutheropolis and is crucified on a tree at a time of persecution. A fisherman Jonas is her third husband and the father of Simeon. Mary Cleophas is a vivacious, attractive woman with a distinguished appearance. She is eager for her sons to be in Jesus' service and speaks to Him about that possibility. He assures her that in time, they will all follow Him (ACE 1 332, 366). The four older sons receive baptism from John at Ainon, and follow him until his death. They later follow Jesus. James the Less, son of Alpheus, eventually becomes the first Bishop of Jerusalem (ACE 3 5).

Jesus is traveling to various places with some of the disciples, teaching and healing many. Then at Matthew's place He spends the night in prayer. In the morning He receives word that Mary Cleophas is quite ill, and His mother urges Him to come to Peter's near Capernaum. Jesus continues with His work and proceeds to Bethsaida where He rests and dines. Mary Cleophas' sons go at once to see their sick mother. Finally Jesus proceeds to Peter's house outside Capernaum and cures many sick people gathered there. The widow of Naim, Maroni, asks Mary Cleophas, who lives at Cana, to go with her to her relative Peter's house, and Mary brings Simeon, her eight–year–old son, with her. When she arrives, she has a fever which continues to increase. Jesus has such great crowds that He continues to teach and heal. The next morning He teaches at the synagogue before a huge crowd. Again His mother sends word that her niece is very ill, and little Simeon quite upset. His father Jonas, recently deceased, is a brother to Peter's father-in-law.

At last Jesus arrives at His cousin's bed, where He prays and places His hands upon her. She is quite exhausted. Jesus takes her by the hand and tells her she is over the sickness. Then He directs someone to bring some food to Mary Cleophas. This calling for food is a common practice at a healing by Jesus. Emmerich realizes it has some relationship to the Blessed Sacrament. The sons are greatly relieved, especially little Simeon as he sees his mother get up and helps other sick people (ACE 3 49–56).

During the last days, Mary Cleophas, Martha, and Magdalen receive the Blessed Sacrament (ACE 4 424). The holy women are nearby in another area during the Last Supper. Jesus comes to them afterward and meets with His mother, Mary Cleophas, and Magdalen. They urge Him not to go to the Mount of Olives for fear the rumors are true of His imminent arrest there. He attempts to comfort them and leaves with the Apostles. A little later Martha, Mary Salome, and a second Salome join the other holy women and go toward the house of Mary Marcus. On the way they meet Lazarus, Nicodemus, Joseph of Arimathea, and some relatives. Mother Mary tells them that Judas left the hall early, behaving suspiciously. The men try to relieve the women's worries, and they continue to Mary Marcus' house (ACE 4 77, 88).

Mary Heli, Mary Cleophas, and Magdalen stand at the foot of the cross with the Virgin Mary (ACE 4 267). These same women follow immediately behind the litter bearing Jesus' body (ACE 4 339). The niece is among a group of four holy women who go to the city for ointments, herbs, nard water, and other aids to take to the tomb for the body of Jesus (ACE 4 360, 365). In the early dawn they return to the tomb with their purchases.

After Jesus arises, He appears to Luke and Cleophas (a grandson of Mary Cleophas' paternal uncle) while they are traveling along the road talking about their doubts and the crucifixion. They do not recognize Jesus but end up having cake and honey together at a public place. Jesus prays, blesses the shining morsels, and places them in their mouths. Jesus disappears, and the men hug very emotionally after they finally recognize Jesus. They head back to Jerusalem (ACE 4 380).

When Jesus appears to the Apostles and several disciples at the place of the Last Supper, Mary Cleophas and Magdalen stand with Mother Mary outside of the hall. Jesus takes the fish and honey—left over from the Last Supper—and gives some to the Apostles, some to a few of the disciples (not all of them), and small portions to the three women (ACE 4 383).

Emmerich tells of seeing the various actions of the Apostles, disciples and others after the crucifixion and after seeing the risen Christ. She relates that Mother Mary is in Bethany. She is quiet, subdued, and serious, more in holy awe than sorrowing. Her niece Mary Cleophas is with her and is exceptionally kind and amiable. She gently tends to Mary and quite tenderly consoles her. Emmerich gives the niece a wonderful compliment, saying she is more like the Virgin Mary than any other woman (ACE 5 389).

Chapter 3

Anna's Ancestors

*A*nna, the grandmother of Jesus, has many ancestors who are Essenes, a sect of Jews who expect the Messiah and dedicate themselves to prepare a channel for the coming of this Messiah. Because it is important that the Messiah come from the line of David, genealogy is a relevant factor. Anna's father is a descendent of Levi, and her mother is a descendent of Benjamin (ACE 5 59). There are many blood relationships among the holy women, Apostles, and disciples who aid at the time prior to Jesus' birth and on through His life and His ministry.

At the time of Anna's grandparents, Stolanus and Emorun (which means noble mother), the superior of the Essenes is Archos, a prophet (ACE 1 120). Before marrying, Emorun consults Archos on Mt. Horeb. By praying and holding the rod of Aaron in his hand, Archos determines that the marriage to Stolanus is a helpful step toward the desire of the Essenes to provide a channel for the Messiah. The rod produces a bud at the end signifying that the marriage is desirable and that a chosen daughter will be among the offspring. The couple has three daughters: Emerentia, Ismeria, and Enue. When they are of marriageable age, they consult Archos. Emerentia marries Aphras, a Levite, and to them is born

___, the mother of John the Baptist. Also, according to Edgar Cayce (1000–14), Elizabeth has a daughter named Adahr, sister of John the Baptist, or Elias as he is called. He is not called John the Baptist until after his death. Her brother's rejection of the teachings in the temple and his acceptance of the Essenes' teachings confuse the sister. She does not like the way her brother dresses in a lamb skin.

Elizabeth appears in a life reading that tells of her being a chosen vessel to be the mother of John the Baptist (2156–1). Also, the reading refers to her having a later life as Celia in the early Roman church. Celia is noted for her service, healing ability, musical ability, and many other qualities that lead to her becoming St. Cecilia.

Enue, the third daughter of Emorun, marries, is widowed, and then is present in Anna's house when Mary is born. Ismeria, the second daughter, has the desired bud on the rod of Aaron and marries Eliud, a Levite. They are wealthy, have property in Sephoris and the valley of Zabulon, but give nearly all to the poor. Sobe is their first daughter. She marries Solomon, and their daughter is Mary Salome who marries Zebedee. Mary Salome is Mary's niece. Zebedee and Mary Salome become the parents of the future Apostles James the Greater and John. We do not know the name of James' wife (1981–1). She is one of the girls in training at the temple and is third on the stair when the angel designates Mary as the channel for the Messiah. According to the Cayce readings, Roael is Zebedee's oldest son and the bridegroom in the wedding at Cana (5749–15). Further, Cayce tells a girl named Clana that she is the bride at the wedding where Mary's son, Jesus, transforms water into wine (609–1).

Naomi is the name of a daughter of Zebedee, born between James and John (540–1,4). Her mother, Mary Salome, is the niece of Anna, mother of the Virgin Mary. Naomi receives her education in the school at Carmel but also associates with people in the temple. She marries at thirty–four and apparently is influenced to do so from associations made at the wedding in Cana. Cayce gives her credit for being one who meditates, sings beautifully, and is an excellent housekeeper.

One other person in Zebedee's family who appears in a Cayce reading is Zebedee's sister Ersa, who becomes acquainted with Luke after the crucifixion (2799–1).

Still the daughter of promise does not come to Ismeria and Eliud until after much prayer and sacrifice; so eighteen years after Sobe's birth, Anna arrives. At the age of five, Anna goes to the temple for twelve years of training. During that time, a third daughter, Maraha, is born; and Sobe has a son named Eliud. When she is nineteen, Anna marries Joachim, also called Heli. He is a relative of St. Joseph and a descendent of David. Ismeria dies, and Anna and Joachim go to live with her father Eliud. Mary Heli is born to them but is not the promised channel. When Mary Heli is seven, Anna and Joachim leave her living with her grand-father and move to another house. Her parents love her, but people criticize them for not taking her with them. Perhaps they feel it best to leave her with her grandfather as they are quite distressed because they have not produced the promised channel. They pray, do penance, and seek solitude. After the priests refuse Joachim's offering at the temple because he has no more children, he leaves for Mt. Horeb to tend his sheep (not advising Anna of his destination). During his five-month absence, both are praying and meditating. Anna is quite concerned about Joachim's whereabouts. Then they both receive messages from angels telling them to meet under the Golden Gate at the temple.

Emmerich relates all of these scenes in great detail (ACE 1 132-138). Joachim arrives at the temple, goes with the priests, who are told by angels to welcome Joachim. The priests take Joachim with them to the Holy of Holies. They leave, and an angel arrives, takes a shining sub-stance from the Ark of the Covenant, and places it beneath Joachim's robe on his chest. After a period of ecstasy, Joachim follows the priests to the subterranean passage beneath the temple. Angels accompany him. Meanwhile Anna, also accompanied by angels, comes toward Joachim in the passageway. The immaculate conception of Mary occurs when the two meet in an ecstatic state and embrace. Both Emmerich and Cayce declare Mary and Jesus to be immaculately conceived. Through the visions of the nun, we begin to understand how this is possible and why these two must enter the world without the taint of sin.

Studying the two sources provides enlightenment on several mys-teries. Emmerich's visions cause us to feel we are observing the scenes she often feels that she is actually interacting with the vision and comments on the strange feeling that she is outside of time. We see the angels fall because of selfishness. We comprehend the creation of Adam as God's plan to guide us back to oneness with God. The nun vividly describes the creature that so successfully convinces Eve to eat of the tree of the knowledge of good and evil. We relate to the pain of Adam and Eve as they leave the garden and take up residence in the very cave where later Jesus fervently prays for the redemption of mankind. The nun bemoans His rejection as the Redeemer by so many of the chosen people, who do not understand that He replaces the Ark and its holy substance, which is the symbol for the son of man. She tells that Jesus prophesizes great suffering for those who reject Him and the opportunity to return to the original state through His sacrifice. Fortunately, many do accept the grace offered. Because the well-organized sects of Jewry seek an earthly messiah who will retain the ego-laden leaders of these groups, Jesus offers His gift to the Gentiles and the pagans. Emmerich's visions are full of such heartwarming incidents.

Chapter 4

The Inns for Jesus' Ministry

On a trip to Tyre with Jesus, Saturnin has to beg for food. The hard crusts require soaking in water to be edible. Innkeepers have been warned by Pharisees not to give shelter or food to Jesus and His followers. This incident is the culmination of many hardships. It inspires the holy women and Lazarus to think of preparing private inns. By supplying them and caring for them or arranging for caretakers to keep them ready as needed, they can help Jesus and His followers as they travel. The men can tell the women in advance what route is to be taken, when, and how many will be traveling. Then the men will no longer have to worry about food and lodging. The women list items needed for the inns: furniture, clothes, sandals, bread and other food, and facilities for washing and making repairs (ACE 2 171-8).

About an hour past Sichar, Jesus—with Andrew, Phillip, Saturnin, and John—arrive at an area with many shepherd huts. One of these shepherd houses is being established as a private inn, which the holy women of Capernaum will prepare and maintain. Mother Mary, Mary Cleophas, the wife of James, and two widows have been preparing everything all day and have the food and flasks of balsam ready to serve dinner. Jesus extends both hands to His mother; the other women bow their heads and cross their hands over their breasts. Mary asks her Son to cure a little lame boy at this place, and He does, much to the joy of the parents and child (ACE 2 192–3).

On another occasion, Jesus goes near Bethsaida. He does not enter that city but goes to Peter's house. The holy women are there, and Peter's wife is with them. Jesus talks at length with the women about a house being arranged as an inn on the lake's borders—a place Jesus will probably frequent often. He tells the women not to be extravagant and not to be anxious about things because he needs little. They are to prepare for the disciples and the poor (ACE 2 222–3).

Lazarus is responsible for building an inn at Meroz, where he owns some land. It has beautiful fields and orchards. Some servants live here in order to care for the fruit and sell it and act as caretakers of the inn. The holy women come in advance of Jesus and His disciples to have all prepared for their two–day stay. Judas Iscariot comes to the inn, and Simon and Bartholomew commend Judas to Jesus, who sighs and looks troubled. During the evening meal, Jesus instructs. Judas, who is a polished man of about twenty–five, does not spend the night; the next night, however, he does stay. It is the first night Judas and Jesus sleep under the same roof (ACE 2 419–431).

The holy women are very conscientious in caring for the inns and keeping them well supplied with such things as linens, woolen clothes, sandals, cups, balsam, and oil. Jesus tells the women he doesn't want the disciples to be a burden to others and wants their needs supplied. That way, the Pharisees will not have an excuse to reproach them (ACE 3 96).

Martha and Susanna act as general superintendents of the inns, and they visit the inns from Galilee to Samaria. They load pack animals with necessities of all kinds to supply the various inns (ACE 3 95). On one occasion, Martha spends time with Magdalen urging her to attend an instruction Jesus is giving in Nazareth. Afterward she goes to the inn near Damna to be with the holy women. About a dozen holy women are there with the Blessed Virgin. Some of them are Mary Marcus, Maroni, Mary the Suphanite, Anna Cleophas, Susanna Alpheus, Susanna of Jerusalem, Seraphia (Veronica), and Johanna Chusa. As these women travel together to Azenoth, they meet Jesus, Lazarus, six Apostles, and several disciples going from the Dothain inn to Azanoth (ACE 3 125). There is a private inn In Dothain for Jesus and His disciples. Lazarus is here from Jerusalem, bringing two of Jesus' disciples and some of the holy women with him. Jesus and His disciples all meet at the inn (ACE 3 122).

Abran is a city of various sects of Jews. Lazarus establishes an inn a quarter of an hour south of the city. An Essenian married couple acts as caretakers. Their children are grown. They descend from Zachariah who was killed between the temple and the altar (not the husband of Elizabeth). The wife is a granddaughter of a sister of Anna. The couple has fields and meadows in the area where Joachim tended sheep, prayed, and meditated during the five months Anna did not know his whereabouts (ACE 3 14).

The holy women never stay at public inns. While they are in Dothan now, near Samaria they stay with an elderly man, Issachar, whom Jesus recently healed. There are twelve holy women here: Martha, Maroni, Dina, Anna Cleophas, Mary Johanna Marcus, Susanna Alpheus, Mary the Suphanite, Magdalen, Susanna, Seraphia (Veronica), and Mary. They go in pairs to check the supplies at inns in their districts and see to it that necessities do not run low. Later they will meet Jesus and His disciples at the shepherd–house inn—the site of previous meetings (ACE 3 143).

Jesus sends his Apostles (with the exception of Peter and John) with some disciples in pairs from the mountain base near Thabor. They are divided into three groups to go in three different directions. They are to travel light: no money, one robe only, and a staff. Because there are many private inns in many of the areas where these men are traveling, their needs will be met in the inns. Those traveling in areas not so blessed with inns will take some money. They are venturing into some new territory. Jesus clarifies His instructions for curing the sick, blesses the healing oil they are carrying, blesses them, and then tells them where they will next meet (ACE 3 140).

Previously Jesus had only thirty–six disciples. The number has now increased to seventy. The holy women count thirty-five in their group. The number of those serving the Community is at least seventy—including the maid-servants, inn directresses, and stewardesses (ACE 3 226).

In Dan, a town at the base of a mountain, Jesus and the thirty Apostles and disciples with Him, settle into an inn located in the middle of the city. It is an inn set up by the disciples themselves on their last mission to Dan. A Jewish elder of the city, a Nazarite, is a friend of Lazarus and Nicodemus and secretly follows Jesus. He is a wealthy man and a big contributor to the holy women in their inn project (ACE 3 234).

Jesus and His disciples take an eighteen-hour trip from Tirzah to Capernaum. They stay at the inn beside the lake near Bethulia. The next day, they go to Damna, where Mary is already present with several of the holy women. Here, six Apostles and more disciples join Jesus. They continue traveling until evening. The disciples and Apostles separate from Jesus and the women, who, with His relatives, go to Mary's house in the Capernaum Valley. Jairus comes to Jesus to tell Him he belongs entirely to Jesus now, as he has lost his office (ACE 3 206-7).

The Apostles and disciples come down the mountain and join Jesus. He speaks of his coming arrest as they walk along. They go to the prepared inn in Bethsaida where they receive a welcome and washing of feet. None of the holy women appear here (ACE 3 267-8).

At the time, the holy women are at the foot of the mountain near Gabara, preparing another inn for Jesus and His Apostles. Jesus spends the day and evening teaching the crowd. Many Pharisees, Sadducees, Herodians, scribes, and magistrates attend the instruction. Jesus places the disciples close to Him in front of these groups, which displeases the Pharisees. He openly warns the disciples against this sect and false prophets and speaks so long with no rest that His voice weakens. Finally, He goes to the inn located on property formerly owned by Magdalen. Awaiting Him are Lazarus, Martha, Dina, Mary the Suphanite, Maroni, His mother, and many Gallilean women. They have brought many provisions, materials, and clothing. After a frugal meal for Jesus and the disciples, the poor receive all the things brought (ACE 3 318-20).

Jesus comes back from Cyprus and tells the Levites that many Jews from Cyprus are coming to Palestine to escape the pagan influence and reconnect with their own people. When He and some disciples go to Naim, several other disciples greet them. The son of the Widow of Naim, Martial—a man who Jesus raised from the dead also greets them. Now twelve disciples attend Jesus while others travel from Jerusalem with some of the holy women. The inn at Naim is ready for the group. The widow Maroni, owns the house. The women of the family come out veiled and bow down at the feet of Jesus. Then they all go into a large hall. Besides the widow, five other women come and sit on a low type sofa: Mary the Suphanite, Magdalen, Martha, Seraphia (Veronica), and Johanna Chusa. When Jesus speaks to them, they respond in turn, telling Him about events in Jerusalem and Herod's action to cause trouble for Jesus and the followers. When they get quite animated, Jesus reminds them that they are judging others. He then tells them about Cyprus and those who are choosing to follow Him (ACE 3 435–38).

At times when groups of holy women gather and have spare time, they do much work for the Community, especially by sewing. They maintain storerooms from which the Apostles and disciples supply their own needs and also provide for the poor. If a need exists in an area, they sew for poor synagogues. Usually the maid–servants, who precede or follow them, carry the materials needed for the finished products. If the stay is extended, the maids go back to other inns and wait for the holy women to return there. Of course, many times the women can attend instructions Jesus gives, but they sit apart and do not mingle with the men.

After the raising of Lazarus from the dead with so much reaction resulting, Jesus takes three young men: Eliud, Silan, and Eremenzear with Him to areas inhabited mostly by pagans and idol worshipers. They also venture to the lands of the Wise Men. The youths swear to Jesus that they will keep the mission secret. Thus, the curiosity of the Apostles is never satisfied, and the Bible contains nothing of His trip. Next, he heads toward Ephron with these three youths in order to go to a rented inn not far from Jericho where he is to meet the holy women. At Ephron, he visits individual houses, healing many sick people. Then He sends the three young disciples to meet the ten holy women already at the Jericho inn. They include Mother Mary, Martha, Magdalen, two others not named, Peter's wife and step-daughter, Andrew's wife, and Zacheus's wife and daughter. Peter, Andrew, and John meet Jesus on the way, and they walk together to Jericho. After the foot washing, the men have a meal; the women eat alone. They all go to a school in Jericho where Jesus instructs. The women are present, too, in a separate section. After the lesson, the holy women go back to the inn, and the following day return to their homes. Jesus and the disciples go to Nazareth (ACE 3 582-3).

Chapter 5

Martha, Silent Mary, and Mary Magdalene: Sisters of Lazarus

*E*mmerich's visions contribute a wealth of information about this extremely interesting family. The parents are very wealthy. The father Zarah is of noble Egyptian ancestry. He once lived in Syria and held a position under the king. Then as a reward for war service, the Roman Emperor granted him land near Jerusalem and in Galilee—so much land that he is like a wealthy prince. The mother Jezabel is a wealthy Jewess Pharisee, and Zarah becomes a Jew and maintains the strict rules of the sect. Zarah gives some of his land to the temple. He possesses a huge castle in Bethany. The family knows of the prophecies of Simeon and Anna and are acquainted with the holy family.

Fifteen children are born to Zarah and Jezebel; six die quite young, and by the time Jesus is teaching, only four are living. Of these four Lazarus is oldest, Martha two years younger, Silent Mary four years younger than her brother, and Magdalen (the name used by Emmerich and in this book) comes nine years after Lazarus. Silent Mary is practically unknown and considered a simpleton, but Jesus knows her and values her as Emmerich shows us (ACE 1 375).

Once, while Jesus walks with Eliud, the devout, elderly Essenian, Jesus confides in him prophecy information about Lazarus and his sisters. He explains that the good and pious Martha and her brother will follow Him. Their sister Silent Mary is highly spiritual, is without sin, but, for the benefit of her soul, she is unable to interact with this world. She lives secluded, though capable of comprehending great mysteries. Her life will be short. Lazarus and Martha will give all their possessions to the Community. Mary Magdalene has taken a wrong turn in life, but she will repent and become even more spiritual than Martha (ACE 1 375).

Magdalen, the youngest, is a beautiful child. She is adored and spoiled by her mother and the maids. They dress her lavishly and display her to an admiring crowd so that she develops into a very vain, self-centered, proud, pleasure-loving being at a very early age. Her parents die when she is only seven, and she has no one to direct her away from undesirable character traits. Naturally, she attracts the attention of males at a very early age, and she quickly learns the arts of seduction. She gains the Madalum property by lot when the family estate is divided during her eleventh year. The property is fortified and consists of several castles, some public buildings, and beautiful groves and gardens. The location of the property is eight hours east of Nazareth, three from Capernaum, less than two hours from Bethsaida to the south, and a short distance from the Lake of Genesareth. Herod is owner of one castle, and some of his soldiers reside on the property. Other officials and servants account for about two hundred people in Magdalum. Magdalen is well known to the military officers. She has many servants and large fields and herds, but without management and maintenance, the place soon deteriorates (ACE 1 334-6). There is much more to say about Magdalen, but the story of her sister Silent Mary is short and strange to the worldly wise.

Perhaps Silent Mary is somewhat like an autistic person. She keeps to her rooms and her private garden and receives care from servants. She is very obedient and polite, cares for her wardrobe, keeps things orderly, and sometimes she and Martha sit together and sew or embroider. She doesn't make appearances, but when someone is around she is silent. Alone, she talks to herself and the objects in view. She is quite pious and prays in her private area. In her visions Emmerich witnesses Mary having visions of her own and talking to apparitions. Jesus understands that her love for her brother and sisters, especially Magdalen, is unspeakable.

Jesus comes and requests of Lazarus a visit with Silent Mary. They go to Martha's place, and Martha brings the veiled Mary to an interior garden where Jesus waits. Martha withdraws. Mary is tall and beautiful and looks upward. She stands mute, and Jesus takes her walking around the garden. They do not really have a conversation. Mary gazes heavenward and speaks of things she seems to see on a different level of existence. It is as though both are seeing a vision regarding Jesus' life, and Mary is speaking aloud of what she sees: the Virgin, the Son as the Redeemer, and the angels singing. Then she speaks to the Virgin and comments that, had the Virgin refused to be the Mother of the Lord, Israel would have suffered long. Then she speaks words of praise and thanksgiving, and now and then Jesus joins in or praises His Father for His mercy. Mary returns to her rooms, and Jesus goes to Lazarus and Martha. Jesus comments that Mary's soul understands the other realm but that she doesn't live in this world and those living in this world do not comprehend her. She is without sin. Jesus is one with whom she communes interiorly. She cannot relate to people who cannot relate with her on the spiritual plane. She seems to be doing penance for the sins of others (ACE 1 402).

At a second interview, Lazarus honors Jesus' request and brings Mary to Him. This time she bows to His feet and kisses them. Jesus raises her by His hand, and she begins to utter wonderful prophecies of what she is seeing on another level of consciousness. She speaks allegorically of the treatment given by the servants to the Son the Father sends to them. The Son pays all the debts but is badly received. He will have to suffer, bleed, and die to redeem His Kingdom so that these ungrateful servants might become the children of the Father. She grieves and rejoices in turn. She speaks of the resurrection and refers to the Son going to the hidden prisons to set the prisoners free and return them to the Father, while also judging the abusers. She tells of Lazarus' death and return after His friend weeps. She refers to Magdalen in a terrible desert like the children of Israel but says that she will come to another desert at last and repent for her past. Mary refers to herself as trapped in her body prison, longing to go home. She feels all are blind and that she does not deserve better. Jesus speaks kindly to her and tells her that very soon He will come again and set her free. He raises His hands and blesses her. Then He anoints her for death and pities her since people consider her a simpleton not worthy of embalming. People cannot see her holiness. She is a holy woman who also serves simply by waiting (ACE 1 484–5).

During Jesus' temptations, Emmerich sees Silent Mary witnessing the temptations and receiving food from the angels. She sees Mary lying on the ground, more aware of this world and her surroundings. Her maids support her in their arms. She realizes that Jesus the Redeemer has come to Bethany, and that He will soon suffer cruelly. Jesus appears. She recognizes Him and has use of her senses. Jesus comforts her and speaks of the Kingdom of God and His own Passion. He blesses her and leaves (ACE 2 113).

When the Pharisees look for Jesus at the home of Mary Marcus in Jerusalem, they find His mother and other women and order them to leave the city. Upset they go to Martha's house in Bethany. Martha is with her sick sister, Mary, who is again out of the conscious world, suffering the pain of Jesus' passion. She dies in the presence of the Blessed Virgin, Mary Cleophas, Martha, and the other women (ACE 2 122). Magdalen goes to Bethany and spends the night weeping for her sister. Martha finds Magdalen, quite distraught, the next morning on Silent Mary's grave. The women of Jerusalem take Magdalen back with them, and, though unaccustomed to walking, she insists on doing so, causing her tender feet to bleed. She goes to Jesus to express her gratitude, weeping at His feet. Jesus speaks kindly to her and advises her to do penance as her sinless sister did. Magdalen then goes to her home with her maid (ACE 3 160).

In the 1930s three people received readings from Edgar Cayce that relate to Lazarus, Martha, and Mary Magdalene. On January 8, 1931, a fifty-five-year-old man receives the information that he lived as Lazarus in Palestine while Jesus walked the earth (1924-1). He is, in that past life, a very close friend of the Master—so close, that, when he dies, Jesus weeps, and calls him from death's arms to continue his life as Lazarus.

On September 30, 1931, a forty-five-year-old woman gets a reading telling her that she walked with the Master in the Promised Land as Martha, a sister to Lazarus and Mary Magdalene (560-1). She gains much and gives much as Martha. She is perhaps a bit too secular in her practicality but understands the power of seeking through love, which she manifests in her home in Bethany.

On December 23, 1929, a twenty-six-year-old woman learns in a reading that she is a sister of Martha and Lazarus during the time that the Master walked the earth (295-1). He tells her she chooses the "good part" (Luke 10:42), and that wherever the gospel is presented in the world, what Mary did shall "be told for a memorial of her" (Matthew 26:13). Further, the reading tells her that, only to aid others, did she come into the present experience. This lady, Mildred Davis, is a cousin to Gladys Davis, Edgar Cayce's longtime secretary.

Another reading, given August 31, 1933, focuses on the life of Mary Magdalene. She first meets Jesus as she appears before the council on the charge of adultery. The council adheres to the law and orders her stoned. Jesus rescues her (John 11:8) and tells her he does not condemn her, but "Go and sin no more." The reading describes Mary as a courtesan involved with Roman officers. In answer to a question about the authenticity of the book, *Under Pontius Pilate,* by William Schuyler, published in 1906 by Funk, the answer is "In the main, authentic." The reading describes Mary's height as about five feet four inches tall, weight about 121 pounds, with almost red hair and blue eyes. She is twenty-three when Christ clears her of seven devils, including avarice, hatred, self-indulgence, selfishness, hopelessness, and blasphemy. The home of Mary and Martha becomes a center of activity after the crucifixion for those other than the Galileans. Jesus appears to Mary first at the resurrection, and she is present at His ascension, which is fifty days later.

Then, years later, Cayce gives a reading for Ulai, who is a cousin of Lazarus and his sisters, and the daughter of Archaus, an Essene, and Josada, a close associate of Jezebel (mother of Lazarus and siblings). She cannot see how someone who lives as Mary does can be so well treated by her brother and sister. When Lazarus dies of typhoid, Ulai comes as a family mourner and connects with Mary and Martha. She feels kinship with Jesus when He weeps at Lazarus' death. She then becomes acquainted with Jesus' mother, becomes one of the holy women, and helps Mother Mary make her home with John. She takes an active part in the church of Laodicea and gets involved in the dispute over Lucius. Later she becomes the companion of Pathaos, a leader in the Antioch Church. In the reading, she receives the advice that in her present life she not dwell on people's faults: "It is not what one once did that counts, but what one *will* do about that it knows to do today!" (993–5)

Lazarus is a very dear friend of Jesus, and when they meet, Jesus often embraces Lazarus, whereas with most other persons, usually a grasp of the hands suffices. Lazarus is probably about eight years older than Jesus. He is a tall man—gentle, serious and confident. He has black hair and is distinguished looking. His house in Jerusalem is on the west side of Mount Sion, near Mount Calvary. Martha owns the castle in Bethany where both of them love to be so that generally Lazarus resides there, too. Since it is quite a large complex, Martha has a house on one side of the courtyard, and Lazarus resides on the opposite side (ACE 1 396). Jesus is coming, and Nicodemus, John Marc, Simeon's son, and a brother or nephew of Anna the Prophetess—all secret friends of Jesus—await with Lazarus, the honored guest. Waiting with Martha in her house, are Seraphia (Veronica), Mary Marcus, and an older woman of Jerusalem (probably Susanna, as she is called by that name later), whom Mary knew in the temple. Jesus tells Martha that His mother is coming to await His baptism by John. The women go to an antechamber in Lazarus' house, where they eat separately from the men. Jesus prays and blesses the food. He tells those assembled that a time of trial is approaching in which He and they will suffer. He urges them to stand by Him.

Emmerich is amazed that none really understand Jesus' words. The men think He is the Messiah, but they believe He will set up an earthly kingdom with His disciples in Jerusalem and rid the Jews of the Roman domination. Then the nun realizes that in her visions she sees all from the fall to the immaculate conception and much more than these present know or misunderstand. They do not comprehend that this is a world of penance and that the Kingdom Jesus refers to is not on this earth. After Mother Mary arrives and Jesus talks privately with her, Martha speaks to Jesus about Magdalen's situation and the concern she has for her sister. Jesus tells her to keep praying for Magdalen and urging her to change, and, in time, she will be converted.

Shortly afterward Jesus goes to John the Baptist to be baptized. Following the baptism, while Jesus stands in prayer on the stone, a rushing wind sounding like thunder comes. Then a bright light shines around a winged being, and a heavenly apparition of God declares, "This is My beloved Son in whom I am well pleased" (ACE 1 441).

After various travels, Jesus goes to an inn near Great Chorazin where He is to meet His mother and some of the holy women who have rented the inn and prepared it at their expense. Susanna of Jerusalem, Peter's wife, and other holy women are present. Jesus privately tells His mother He will go to Bethany and then to the desert. She is concerned. Jesus speaks to crowds of people from the surrounding countryside. There are about thirty women present, who stand separately. After the crowd departs, Jesus tells His followers that He is soon leaving for a time and that they and the women are to disband until He returns.

Jesus leaves with about twenty followers and arrives at an inn near Aruma. Martha, making her first trip with the holy women, prepares this inn, while friends in Jerusalem fund expenses. Lazarus goes with Jesus to the inn near the desert. Jesus goes alone to a grotto near Jericho after telling Lazarus He will return after forty days.

The nun has amazing visions of Jesus in the desert being tempted by Satan. She sees many interesting things happening to friends of Jesus at that time and in the future. She sees angels minister to Jesus in the desert by carrying wine and bread to Him. Angels also ministered to Mother Mary at Cana, Lazarus and Martha, Mary the Silent, who is actually witnessing Jesus' desert temptations and suffering, and Magdalen who feels a strange longing for a different life (ACE 2 18).

Shortly after the forty–day desert fast, Jesus goes with Martha, Johanna Chusa, Simeon's son, and Lazarus toward Cana. Nathanael, the son of a daughter of Anna's sister Sobe, is the bridegroom of Cana where

Jesus turns water to wine at His mother's urging (ACE 2 34).

Martha urges Magdalen to go with her to Jezrael to hear Jesus. Magdalen agrees to go, but Jesus cures many people near the synagogue and then leaves in a few hours. When the sisters arrive, people tell them of their being cured, but they cannot find Jesus. Magdalen gets separated from Martha and goes back to Magdalum. Shortly after this incident Jesus and Lazarus are together. They speak of Magdalen, and Jesus tells Lazarus that Magdalen's soul is now moved by a touch of salvation, which will entirely take hold of her (ACE 2 72).

Among other places that Jesus goes next is Phasael, where an Essenian named Jairus (of the line of Chariot) lives. He pleads with Jesus to come heal his daughter, and Jesus promises he will, but she dies before He gets there. Upon His arrival, He opens the winding sheet, takes the teenage girl by her hand, and commands her to rise up. She does. She is a girl with no love for a father who is pious and generous, but she means the world to him. Jesus awakens her body and soul so that she changes completely and joins the holy women. There is another Jairus in Capernaum with a daughter that Jesus also raises from the dead at a later time (ACE 2 78).

From Phasael Jesus goes again to Jezrael. The disciples from Galilee meet Him here along with other men. Martha, Johanna Chusa, Seraphia (Veronica) convince Magdalen to go to Jezrael again if only to see Jesus. She comes along, her vanity undisguised. While she is at the window of the inn, Jesus and His disciples pass by. Jesus looks at her quite piercingly so that she feels confused on the soul level. She seeks a place to hide from this all-knowing gaze and runs into a house of refuge for lepers and other sick women who stay in a semi-hospital environment. She feels the misery of her state because she comes here out of pride, with respectful women. She returns to Magdalum with Lazarus, Martha, and the other women (ACE 2 79). They leave Magdalum and head to Mother Mary's house to see her before going on to Jerusalem. Jesus arrives and tells Martha that she is too disturbed about her sister. Magdalen's experiences influence her, but she will still not renounce her lifestyle as she is accustomed to dressing to the hilt and does not yet want to change to the modest dress of the holy women (ACE 2 81).

Jesus arrives at Lazarus' house in Bethany, and Martha goes to Jerusalem to invite Mary Marcus and others to come. Seraphia (Veronica), Susanna, Johanna Chusa, and about nine men are present at the dinner. Jesus talks about the nearness of His Kingdom and refers to His suffering to come. The next day, Martha and the other women prepare a meal and take it to Jesus at the house of Obed, the son of Simeon, opposite the temple in Jerusalem (ACE 2 107)

Feeling compassion for Magdalen, James the Greater calls at her home to urge her to attend an instruction Jesus is giving at Gabara. Magdalen receives this impressive and pleasant man in a neighboring house. She has graciously received him on previous visits. James tells her that Jesus is superior to all and that he is sure Magdalen will feel fortunate to hear Him. She need not concern herself about her clothes—ordinary dress will do. Magdalen seems open to accepting the invitation but wavers.

Then Martha and Anna Cleophas make an hour trip from the inn at Damna to see Magdalen. Magdalen receives her sister in a kindly manner, not in her room of state but in a nearby apartment. She is embarrassed by her sister's simple dress, but she also feels some shame because of her manner of living compared to the simple, pious life of Martha. She is not comfortable taking her into the area where she lives so extravagantly. Magdalen looks pale and ruffled partly because of a crude man living with her, who is distasteful to her.

Martha is not aggressive and is affectionate and kind. She tells her sister that two friendly women Magdalen knows, Dina and the Suphanite, are going to hear Jesus, and that the site on the mountain near Gabara is not far. All are eager for her to come and see an interesting gathering, miraculous cures of sick people, and a provocative exchange with the Pharisees. Jesus' mother and other women feel that attending will cheer her up from her forlorn state. All want her with them. Because Magdalen is in a sad state, she listens to Martha and finally promises she will go.

The day comes for the instruction, and the women gather at a spot not far from the teacher's chair. Crowds of the various sects of Jews arrive. Jesus takes the chair with His disciples gathered on one side and the Pharisees on the other. Emmerich declares that this is Jesus' most

powerful sermon yet and goes into a considerable report of the message. He establishes His authenticity, enumerates the sins of the listeners, and warns of the dire consequences of their rejecting Him and His
message. There is an exchange with the Pharisees when Jesus says that
those rejecting His message will fare worse than the inhabitants of
Sodom and Gomorrah. Finally, Jesus relays a message filled with love
for those who come to Him.

Magdalen is hearing all this with an assumed air of self-confidence
but is really struggling interiorly. She finally makes a move to be the
one soul Jesus calls to Him. The women tell her to wait. It is dark when
Jesus finishes and the crowd disperses. The women go to follow Jesus
and the disciples as they attend to the sick. Magdalen moves among the
sick and relates to their misery. She is quite moved by the healings and
the gratitude of the healed. When Jesus comes to heal women—separate
from the men—Magdalen tries to draw near Jesus, but He avoids her.
She is amazed by the human suffering and the healing of ones possessed by unclean spirits, which cause them to hurl themselves about
and scream.

When Jesus and the disciples start down the mountain, even though
this is considered unacceptable conduct, Magdalen follows them as
closely as possible. In order not to be separated, the other women do
the same. More healing follows as Jesus and the disciples make their
way to entertainment planned by the Pharisees. They want to send the
poor away, but Jesus requires them to prepare tables for the poor. The
meal begins with the disciples serving and eating with the poor. Jesus
continues His instructions. Suddenly, Magdalen darts into the hall and
empties the contents of a little flask over Jesus' head. She takes her veil,
folds it and presses it to Jesus' head to absorb the extra ointment. All are
silent. People gaze, glare, and whisper. Jesus speaks and defends
Magdalen, saying she acts out of love and gives honor due a guest. He
says to Magdalen, "Go in peace! Much has been forgiven thee." The
women leave, and Jesus says Magdalen is a woman full of compassion.
He lectures the crowd on public criticism of exterior faults, saying that
the accusers often harbor worse evils in their hearts.

When the women return to their inn, they leave for the inn about an hour distant, near Bethulia, where Jesus' mother and the other holy women await their coming. Magdalen reports on Jesus' sermon while others tell of Magdalen's actions and Jesus' comments. All want Magdalen to go with them to Bethany, but she insists on returning to her home as she has commitments there. This does not please the holy women. Magdalen cannot say enough good words about Jesus and desires to follow Him and join Martha and her friends. Martha goes a way with her sister and maid towards Magdalum and then travels to Capernaum with the holy women.

Very soon Magdalen falls into her old ways as she listens to the men visiting her ridicule Jesus and tell her that she is more beautiful than ever. She suffers cramps and convulsions, indicative of her possessed state (ACE 2 470–484).

After spending the night at Peter's house, Jesus and the disciples go to see Jairus and his family, including the elderly mother, who is very grateful. The daughter that Jesus awakened from death comes when summoned—veiled, humble, and healthy. Next, Jesus goes to see His mother. Martha, Mary Cleophas, Susanna Alpheus, Susanna of Jerusalem, and Dina the Samaritan are with her. Martha is upset because of Magdalen's total relapse and obvious demoniacal possession. When she asks Jesus if she should go to her sister, He tells her to wait awhile. Magdalen is in a terrible state, striking her maids, having fits of anger, and dressing in a shameful manner. She and the man living with her exchange blows. She cries out for the Teacher, meaning Jesus (ACE 3 94).

Martha and Susanna of Jerusalem go to their inns from Galilee to Samaria since they serve as general overseers in this territory while the other women look after the inns in their districts. They take pack animals loaded with provisions to meet the needs of Jesus and those traveling with Him (ACE 3 95).

Martha feels so sad because of Magdalen's fall into old habit patterns. Since Jesus plans to teach at Azanoth, Martha and her maid go to Magdalen's house to persuade her to attend. She receives haughty treatment and Magdalen leaves her waiting. Martha patiently spends the time praying. Finally, Magdalen appears in a defiant mood, criticizes Martha's plain clothes, and wants her to leave before her guests see her.

Martha requests a place to rest and a servant takes her to another building, where the maid and Martha are left without any refreshments or water. Magdalen dresses elaborately for the banquet she is giving and sits in a very ornamented chair.

Finally, she comes to Martha with a little plate of food and drink. She treats Martha with anger and disdain. Martha humbly and lovingly invites her sister to go with her to an instruction Jesus is giving nearby, saying her female friends are attending and are eager to see her. Martha reminds her sister how taken she was with Jesus' previous message and how she had known how to honor Him when others did not. Magdalen treats her sister contemptuously, but Martha patiently and lovingly continues so that at last Magdalen says she will go—only not with Martha.

The next morning Magdalen requests Martha's presence while Magdalen is being dressed and coiffed by her maids. Emmerich—a former seamstress herself—gives a long description of the over-dressing as it occurs. Magdalen wears jewel-encrusted hair, a boldly embroidered undergarment with a robe and boldly patterned mantle.

Martha leaves for the inn at Damna. Mother Mary and about a dozen holy women, including Mary Marcus, Dina, Maroni, the Suphanite, Anna Cleophas, Susanna Alpheus, Susanna of Jerusalem, Seraphia (Veronica) and Johanna Chusa leave for Azanoth. On the way they meet Jesus, several disciples, and six Apostles and continue together.

Meanwhile, Magdalen is tormented by the forces trying to stop her from hearing Jesus. Since some of her guests have agreed to go see the big show as they call it, she rides with them on their donkeys. Extra animals carry her fancy seat, rugs, and coverings for the others. This loud, bold group settles well in front of the holy women, as people— among them the Pharisees who witnessed her anointing of Jesus—look at Magdalen and her entourage with disapproval and indignation.

Jesus begins His instruction. Little children cry out to Him, "Son of David! Son of God!" so that people, including Magdalen, marvel and tremble. Looking at Magdalen, Jesus observes to the crowd that, when devils are driven out of a house, the devils often return with more devils and rage worse than ever. Then, Jesus starts commanding devils to depart from those who want deliverance from demon domination.

Voices cry out acknowledging Jesus as the Son of God. Many fall unconscious, and Magdalen falls into convulsions. This happens three times, and the nun sees dark forms leave her. Her companions try to remove her. Martha hurries to her, but when she regains consciousness, she acts strange, weeping profusely and wanting to go to the holy women. Her companions restrain her and take her down the mountain, where they abandon her to Lazarus, Martha, and others.

Later, they go to a school where Jesus is teaching. Jesus focuses on a veiled Magdalen, and another evil spirit leaves her as she again loses consciousness. When she awakes, she runs through the street, tears her clothes, and hides her face in her veil, saying she is a wicked sinner. The holy women finally quiet her, but when Jesus, some disciples and Pharisees come to the inn for refreshments, Magdalen escapes and casts herself at Jesus' feet begging for salvation. The men are scandalized and tell Jesus she should be sent away. Jesus tells them they do not understand what is passing through her. He tells Magdalen to fully repent in her heart, to believe and hope, and soon peace will come. Martha takes her back to the inn where Magdalen continues to lament.

After his sister calms down, Lazarus agrees to go take charge of her property and break the ties she has in Magdalum. He has already taken charge of fields and vineyards she owns elsewhere.

The next morning, a miserable Magdalen sits among the holy women as Jesus condemns impurity and speaks of God's mercy on those who accept His grace. Three times Jesus glances at Magdalen during His discourse. Each time Emmerich sees dark vapors rise from her. She is scarcely recognizable from her weeping and emotional stress.

When Jesus ends His instructions, His mother, Martha, and Jesus take Magdalen to a secluded place where she can privately confess her sins to Jesus who comforts her, forgives her, and promises to save her from another relapse. He extols His mother's virtues in a way Emmerich has not heard before. Jesus urges Magdalen to learn from Mother Mary and seek her advice and consolation. Later, Magdalen seeks forgiveness from each of the holy women as they affectionately comfort her. She is too weak to travel on with the group. Therefore, Martha, Mary the Suphanite, and Anna Cleophas stay with her for the night and follow the others the next morning (ACE 3 122–130).

A nephew of Joseph of Arimathea comes from Jerusalem and brings news of Lazarus being ill. While Jesus is at Jericho, messengers from Bethany come to the disciples and tell them that Martha and Magdalen long for Jesus to come to Bethany because of Lazarus' sickness. However, Jesus continues north to a little village where He cures blind men before the disapproving Pharisees. The disciples want Jesus to go to Bethany, not only for Lazarus' sake but because it is a larger place, and they would be less molested by dissenters there (ACE 3 464).

Jesus cures the ten lepers, and only one returns to thank Him (and later becomes a disciple). A shepherd father catches up with Jesus and begs Him to come back to the village with Him as his daughter is dead. Jesus, Peter, John, and James the Greater travel to the village and find that the seven–year–old girl is indeed dead four days. Jesus places one hand on her head and one on her chest. Then He looks up and prays. The child comes back to life. Jesus tells the disciples they can do the same. The grateful father later becomes a disciple (ACE 3 479).

The Blessed Virgin and Mary Cleophas come to spend the Sabbath with Jesus in a place near Samaria. Here they receive word of Lazarus' death in Bethany. Martha and Magdalen leave Bethany after the embalming of Lazarus and go to their house in the country near Ginaea, planning to meet Jesus and the Blessed Virgin there. All the Apostles arrive and go in groups to the house. Jesus' mother is already there. Magdalen comes and exclaims that Lazarus would still be alive had Jesus been there. Jesus answers that His time has not yet come. He then tells Martha and her sister to leave all belonging to Lazarus at Bethany— that He would go there soon. At that, the holy women head to Bethany. The sisters and a messenger come requesting that Jesus come immediately, but he delays. The disciples murmur about His delay, and Jesus scolds them. While He is teaching, the mother of James and John hears Jesus say He is near to fulfilling His mission. She requests that He place her sons, His relatives, in high posts in His Kingdom. He expresses His displeasure with her request.

At last Jesus heads to Bethany where Lazarus lies dead for eight days. He lies dead four days before burial while his sisters hope Jesus will arrive. Martha receives the message from Mary Zebedeus that Jesus comes. Martha goes to find Magdalen in the garden to tell her so that she can speak to Jesus first. Martha goes after Magdalen, who throws herself at Jesus' feet and cries that Lazarus would not have died had Jesus come. All weep, including Jesus. Then He speaks at length about death. The crowd grows and people murmur their disappointment that Jesus did not come in time.

The next morning Jesus, the Apostles, about seven women including Jesus' mother, Magdalen, Martha, and a growing crowd travel the road to the walled-in cemetery. Jesus takes some of the Apostles, and they go down into the vault while the holy women remain by the doorway. People crowd around and climb up wherever they can in order to see. Jesus has the Apostles remove the stone. Martha reminds Him that, after four days in the grave Lazarus, will stink. The outer wrappings come off; Jesus looks upward, and calls, "Lazarus, come forth!" Lazarus sits up. The Apostles remove the napkins, the bindings, and the winding sheet. Lazarus arises resembling a ghost. An Apostle places a mantle about Lazarus, and as he exits the grave, all fall back in fear. The women fall prostrate on the ground. Jesus steps out and grasps Lazarus with both hands in a very loving manner. Lazarus drops to the ground in front of Jesus who speaks some words, and the Apostles, Jesus, and Lazarus go alone into the dining room. Here the Apostles form a circle around the kneeling Lazarus and Jesus. With his right hand on Lazarus' head, Jesus breathes on him seven times. Emmerich describes the breaths as luminous and sees a dark-winged figure leave Lazarus. Jesus consecrates Lazarus to His service, declares him free from the world's sins, and gives him strength with Holy Ghost gifts. He speaks at length to Lazarus and warns him that he will be greatly persecuted by the Jews. Emmerich explains that, while body and soul were separated, Lazarus communicated with several on the other side, including Joseph, Joachim, and Anna, about how the Redeemer is doing on earth. Lazarus changes out of his grave clothes into his regular clothes and embraces his overjoyed sisters and friends. A man serves a meal to the men. The women enter afterward and sit at the lower end of the hall to hear Jesus teach. Because the crowd outside has increased greatly, the Apostles go out to send all away.

Very early the next morning Jesus, John, and Matthew go somewhat disguised to Jerusalem by way of side streets to the house owned by Nicodemus (who had left to go see Lazarus). There He instructs His friends, including Mary Marcus and Seraphia (Veronica) and about twelve men. Emmerich sees that the Pharisees and High Priests later gather and express their fear that Jesus might raise all the dead. About noon that day, a crowd in Bethany seeks Jesus intending to stone Him. The Apostles manage to slip away safely (ACE 3 481–488).

Jesus tells the disciples He will be gone for nine weeks and instructs them about what they are to do and where they are to go while He is gone. Because there are only three youths and no Apostles traveling with Him to pagan areas, none of these travels appear in the Bible. Meanwhile, In Jerusalem many people convert due to the raising of Lazarus (ACE 3 495).

When Jesus returns to the joyful Apostles and disciples, He disperses them again. Since Jesus forbids the three youths to tell the others where Jesus traveled, the three simply continue on with Jesus toward Ephron and then to an inn at Jericho, where they will meet the holy women. There are ten women there, including Martha, Magdalen, and the Blessed Virgin. They kneel before Jesus and kiss His hand. When His mother arises, He kisses her hand. After a meal during which the women eat alone, they go to the end of the hall to hear Jesus teach. After the meal, Jesus, Peter, Andrew, and John (who rejoin Him on the road), go to Jericho. The holy women follow and assist with the gathered sick. When an instruction at a school ends, the women return to their inn. Next morning they return to their homes (ACE 3 581–2).

During the preparation time for the Paschal feast, the disciples walk about in Jerusalem feeling uneasy. Six of the holy women, including Mother Mary, Magdalen, and Martha go to Mary Marcus' house. They hear alarming reports and decide to go into the city for news of Jesus. On the way, they meet Lazarus, Nicodemus, Joseph of Arimethea, and some Hebron relatives. They try to comfort the women and suggest that no attempts will be made on Jesus at this feast time (ACE 4 88).

Nevertheless, Judas betrays Jesus, and the guards arrest Him, bind

Him painfully, and lead Him away. The group of disciples and holy women hear the shouting and noise. One of the Apostles who had been with Jesus advises them of what is happening. The Blessed Virgin, Martha, Magdalen, Mary Cleophas, Mary Salome, Mary Marcus, Johanna Chusa, Seraphia (Veronica), Susanna, and Salome start walking toward the Valley of Josaphat. Lazarus, John Mark, Simeon's son, and Seraphia's son are with them. Mother Mary is internally contemplating Jesus' suffering and allows the holy women to lead her back after the procession passes (ACE 4 126). The women pass through Ophel, and when the people recognize her, they crowd around her in compassion. The women make it to the house of Mary Marcus. Soon, John appears, and Mother Mary asks him questions and grieves. Next they escort her to Martha's house, which is close to Lazarus' house in Jerusalem's west side (ACE 4 130).

Martha next appears in Emmerich's visions at the crucifixion, where she stands with a group of the holy women in the second row behind the Blessed Virgin. Magdalen is in this group, too, totally distraught (ACE 4 267).

While Jesus is on the cross, about forty men from various Jewish sects ride up and around the cross. Seeing the Blessed Virgin, they drive her back calling her a dissolute woman. John takes her to the women standing farther back, and Martha and Magdalen support her, holding her in their arms. The men taunt Jesus. He prays for their forgiveness, and Mary, hearing His voice, presses forward into the circle, followed by John, Salome, and Mary Cleophas. The guard captain does not stop her (ACE 4 284).

At the time of the procession to the tomb, Martha and Lazarus are in Bethany with some of the holy women (ACE 4–339). Later, they return to Jerusalem to keep the Sabbath along with Maroni, Mary the Suphanite, and Dina the Samaritan. They arrive quite late at the apartment of the Blessed Virgin. Many other holy women, numerous disciples, and Apostles, who gradually make their way to the place, are also here. The men gather in a separate area. All are in a state of great distress and mourning (ACE 4 343).

Martha has a very demanding duty during the time of the Disciples' dispersion and Jesus' crucifixion. She is deeply grieving and yet sees to everything and helps in many ways and numerous places. It falls on her to provide food and shelter for many of the wandering and scattered followers. Johanna Chusa, widow of a former servant of Herod, is her main assistant, especially with the cooking (ACE 4 390).

There is a huge gathering in Bethany of about 350 faithful followers—fifty of whom are women who have given all their belongings to the Community. The Blessed Virgin is there, too, and stays with Martha and Magdalen. They hold a love–feast in the open hall of Lazarus' court (ACE 4 410).

The faithful increase and frequently come to the inn of the disciples outside of Bethany, where the disciples take turns dwelling in order to greet, advise, and direct the strangers. The disciples send numerous followers to Lazarus, the owner of many dwellings. Martha and Magdalen give up their Bethany houses to converts. Lazarus turns all that he owns over to the Community. Nicodemus and Joseph of Arimathea do likewise and take over distributing aid and managing Community property (ACE 4 415, 419).

Lazarus receives a very touching farewell from Jesus when He places a shining morsel in Lazarus' mouth, blesses him, and clasps his hand. Then, during the final days before the ascension, Martha, Magdalen, and Mary Cleophas receive the Blessed Sacrament. Women receive baptism after Pentecost. Before Jesus ascends, He tells Magdalen that she is to live concealed in the wilderness while Martha is to establish a women's community, and He says that He will always be with them. Eventually Lazarus, Martha, and Magdalen are imprisoned by the Jews and exiled over the sea (ACE 4 421, 424, 450, 460). In the reading for Mary Magdalene, Cayce explains: "As to Martha's experience then in this period: With the rebellions that arose (that is, the coming of the soldiery that made for the dissension), we find Martha joined with those that brought the rebellion of Saul, and it was under his direction that the persecutions and banishments brought about the death of Martha." (295-8)

The lives of Martha and Magdalen are intricately intertwined. Although we learn much about Magdalen from Martha's story, such as her conversion, the relapse, and the second conversion, there is still much to know about Magdalen.

Emmerich tells of Magdalen's many admirers and how she writes love poems on little rolls of parchment to give to these admirers. However, she never seems to love nor be loved. She has great confidence in her beauty to the point of vanity and self-adoration. She dresses frivolously, and her actions cause embarrassment and pain for Lazarus and Martha. She is ashamed of them because of their simple lives and has no love for them (ACE 1 336). At the time of her first conversion, she is a woman taller than most, quite robust but graceful with lovely tapering fingers, small feet, and a full head of beautiful, long nearly red hair.

After Magdalen's second conversion, she asks Lazarus to take over her estate, which he does. Magdalen moves into the little apartments of her deceased sister, Silent Mary (ACE 3 188). Lazarus puts a steward in charge of Magdalen's property, including the castle. The man living with Magdalen gladly accepts the residence near Gennim that Lazarus offers him (ACE 3 160). Later, Magdalen allows Lazarus to sell much of her property and let Jesus use some of the money to pay the debts of those in debtor prisons. The Herodians often imprisoned people for debts but kept their money—a system that prevented them from paying their debts and leaving jail. The Pharisees accuse Jesus of using women to wage war and ridicule the type of kingdom He can establish with such an army (ACE 3 200). The inn at the foot of the mountain near Gabara, once a part of Magdalen's property, becomes available for use by the Community (ACE 3 319).

After Magdalen starts working with the holy women, she early develops a pattern of embracing Jesus' feet whenever possible. She also frequently anoints His head. Once, she takes Mary Salome, a relative of Joseph, to a shepherd's hut that Lazarus owns some distance from Bethany in hopes of meeting Jesus there. She takes food for Him. When He arrives, she rushes out and embraces His feet. Jesus soon leaves to go to Lazarus' inn closer to Bethany. Magdalen and Mary Salome return home a different way (ACE 3 275).

Jesus reaches Lazarus' house. Lazarus washes His feet, and the veiled women greet Him. They show Jesus the four Paschal lambs that have been decorated with wreaths twined by Jesus' mother and Magdalen. During the meal, Jesus refers to His being the Paschal lamb of His coming Passion. He teaches more on the Sabbath and states clearly that He is the Christ. Magdalen feels more and more penitent and overflows with love and gratitude for Jesus. She follows Him wherever possible. Jesus encourages her transformation. She is a changed person, still noble and distinguished looking, but frequent weeping mars her beauty. She sits alone in a small chamber doing penance. Sometimes she serves the poor and sick by doing lowly services for them (ACE 3 275–6). Later when Jesus is at Naim and several holy women meet Him there, Emmerich remarks that she sees Magdalen and Mary the Suphanite are much less beautiful. Their eyes are red from weeping and they look rather thin and pale (ACE 3 436).

At a Sabbath instruction for Apostles and disciples, about fifteen days before the crucifixion, Jesus foretells many future happenings to those of the Community after His death. Lazarus and the holy women will be persecuted; His mother will go to Ephesus to live. He tells of Simon Magus, who will perform many of the miracles Jesus did but from the devil's power, and much more. Emmerich gives a list of things that will happen three years after the crucifixion including: Mary will go with John to make her home in Ephesus; Jerusalem will be the scene of the persecution of Lazarus, Martha, and Magdalen; Magdalen, prior to that time will do penance in the same cave in the desert to which Elizabeth took John to escape the slaughter of the Innocents; and when Mary dies in Ephesus, the Apostles will all meet for the last time (ACE 4 67).

The Palm Sunday procession is being prepared. Jesus, Peter, John, James, the Blessed Virgin, and six holy women are in the subterranean apartments with Lazarus. All the absent Apostles come to join the others, and Jesus talks at length with them. The eldest disciples go on to Jerusalem to let Mary Marcus and Seraphia (Veronica) and others know that Jesus will soon be approaching. Next, Jesus, the Apostles, and the other disciples start toward Bethphage. Mary leads the holy women some distance behind. At Bethphage a crowd gathers, and Jesus instructs all, including the holy women. Jesus then arranges the Apostles to proceed two by two with Peter first. The holy women, also two by two, bring up the rear, with the Blessed Virgin leading. They all start forward and start singing. The people of Bethphage follow, and a great crowd develops. Several priests in their official garb step into the road and stop the procession. They ask why Jesus is allowing this noise and crowd. Jesus answers that the stones would cry out if the crowd were silenced. The priests leave.

The procession moves on with people laying branches and pieces of clothing in the path. Seraphia (Veronica) and two children come and throw two veils in the way. Then they join the holy women, who number about seventeen at this point. It takes three hours to reach the temple—a trip that ordinarily takes an hour. The priests order all houses and city gates closed, and it is evening before the gates open again. Magdalen worries that Jesus and His followers can have no food in Jerusalem. She prepares a meal for them herself. She washes Jesus' feet when He arrives. Then, while Jesus eats, Magdalen pours balm over His head, much to the disgust of Judas (ACE 4 11–21).

Jesus goes back to Bethany for the Sabbath with the Apostles. The Jews have ordered houses closed and no food to be offered to Jesus. The Apostles and Jesus go to the public house of Simon, the leper healed by Jesus, where a meal awaits. Magdalen meets Jesus at the door, wearing a robe of penitence and a black veil. She casts herself at Jesus' feet and uses her hair to wipe the dust from His feet, which is considered scandalous conduct by many. At the end of the meal, Magdalen appears with a flask of balm, which she pours on Jesus' head and also on His feet, which she then wipes with her hair. This is a fairly common practice of hers, for which she receives much criticism. Jesus acknowledges her gratitude to Him for redeeming her and her consequent love for Him (ACE 4 22).

The holy women serve a large meal at Lazarus' house to Jesus and the Apostles. Jesus says it will be their last meal at Lazarus' but they will gather again at Simons. He answers questions. Thomas has many, and John gently asks some. Jesus tells them it is a beautiful scene when a soul is saved and led home to heaven (ACE 4 26). Judas is out buying provisions for the entertainment at Simons, and Magdalen goes to Jerusalem to have Seraphia (Veronica) buy her three kinds of the best

possible ointment and gives her all the money she has. Magdalen carries the flasks in a pocket under her mantle. She returns to Bethany
accompanied by Mary Marcus. When she gets there, she tells the holy
women that Seraphia (Veronica) tells her she hears that the Pharisees
are going to arrest Jesus as soon as the crowds that follow Him leave
Jerusalem and then put Him to death.

Later, the women are at Simon's house, helping to prepare the provisions which Judas bought. He spent all the money from the purse, be-
lieving he would soon get it all back. The holy women sit at their own
table. Magdalen, in tears, sits opposite Virgin Mary, who carves the
smaller lamb for the women. Meanwhile Jesus carves the larger lamb at
the men's table. He teaches throughout the meal (ACE 4 43, 45).
Magdalen leaves the women and walks to the men's hall. She bends
over Jesus' feet, removes His sandals, and anoints His feet. She moves
her veil enough to use her hair to dry His feet and replaces the sandals.
Jesus tells the men not to be scandalized with Magdalen and softly
speaks to her. She steps behind Jesus and pours costly water over His
head. The fragrant odor fills the room, and Apostles whisper and mut-
ter because of the interruption. Judas grabs at her and scolds her for her
extravagance, but Jesus declares she is anointing Him for His death and
that her action and their disapproval will be preached wherever the
Gospel is told (ACE 4 43–46).

During the time that Jesus prays in great agony in the grotto at
Gethsemane, Satan, unable to comprehend Jesus' divinity, tries every
argument possible to keep Jesus from taking on the sins of the world.
When He accuses Jesus of a crime by distributing the proceeds of
Magdalen's property, Emmerich shouts at Satan and tells him that Jesus
rescued twenty–seven poor prisoners held in the debtors' prison at
Tirzah with that money (ACE 4 85).

The nun recounts another vision of Jesus' agony in the grotto while
Peter, James, and John wait and pray outside. It is of Jesus seeing a
vision of the horrible ingratitude of future generations that causes Him
in His trembling, bleeding state to go out to the three Apostles. They are
shocked at Jesus' state and jump up to support Him. Jesus tells them He
faces death the next day, that within the hour He will be seized, dragged

before the courts, abused, derided, scourged, and put to death in a most horrible manner. He requests them to console His mother. He continues His account of the horrors He will suffer and begs them to give comfort to His mother and Magdalen. Then, at His request, the Apostles help lead Him back to the grotto for more prayer.

The nun also sees the Blessed Virgin at the house of Mary Marcus with Magdalen, too. Mother Mary and the other two are in the garden. Mary is interiorly suffering with Jesus in His agony. She is, therefore, terribly anguished and sorrowful as she kneels in the garden. It is because Jesus sees the suffering of Mary and Magdalen that He makes the request of the three Apostles to comfort the Mother, as she loves Him above all others. He knows Magdalen loves Him most next to His mother and that Magdalen will suffer in the future because of Him and will never again offend Him (ACE 4 103).

Jesus is arrested as he foresaw. His captors mistreat Him terribly. His mother, with Him in spirit, feels all His suffering, but she is very capable of appearing most calm on the exterior. She and Magdalen are certainly contrasts. They, with John, watch as the executioners lead Jesus away. His enemies want Him eliminated so that they can proceed with serving the Paschal lamb. The journey is a torturous one. Mary the Mother gets glimpses of Jesus until He reaches Herod. She begs John and Magdalen to take her over the path that Jesus has just taken. The three go over the whole route together. They pause where Jesus fell. Magdalen wrings her hands. Weeping, John assists the Blessed Mother to her feet after she falls to her knees and kisses the earth wherever Jesus fell. This is the Holy Way of the Cross being traversed by three wholly devoted to Jesus immediately after He creates the path. Magdalen is nearly insane with grief. In her repentance she fully realizes that Jesus is enduring this horrible experience to atone for her sins. Thus, she feels the weight of responsibility, which almost crushes her in her sorrow and gratitude. John has a pure heart and loves without the weight of sin but suffers nonetheless (ACE 4 190, 193).

The nun describes Mary and then contrasts Magdalen while they witness the horrors of Jesus. She says Magdalen is the reverse of the Blessed Virgin. She is taller and more stylish in her figure and her manner. She is not now beautiful because her intense grief and heavy repentance rob her of her former beauty. Her passions are unrestrained so that it is painful rather than pleasant to look at her. Her clothes are wet, torn, and muddy. Her hair is disheveled, and she is totally changed in appearance (ACE 4 225).

At the place of crucifixion, Magdalen is in a totally distraught state. Her grief leaves her reeling as though intoxicated. She is distracted, lamenting, wringing her hands. She moans, threatens the torturers, and has to be concealed and silenced. She requires continual support from the other holy women (ACE 4 267). As the executioners nail Jesus to the cross, Magdalen is nearly insane. She tears at her face with her nails until her cheeks are bloody. Her grief consumes her so that her emotions are violent and out of control. Nothing can calm her as she is oblivious to anything or anyone. Towards the end, she leans at the back of the cross (ACE 4 266, 273, 297, 327).

Joseph of Arimathea and Nicodemus remove Jesus' body from the cross and lay Him in His mother's arms. Magdalen kneels and buries her face in His feet (ACE 4 330). As Mary washes the wounds on the body, Magdalen lends assistance, but she remains mostly at Jesus' feet bathing them with water and tears and drying them with her hair. Her reverence for Jesus keeps her from approaching His face. She presses her face to His feet instead. She is third in the procession to the tomb behind the litter with Jesus' mother and her sister the first two (ACE 4 330-334).

The men and holy women prepare the body with all kinds of herbs. Magdalen takes a flask of balm and empties it into the wound in Jesus' side. Also, Magdalen gathers flowers and branches in the garden, and when Mary leaves the burial cave, Magdalen scatters them over Jesus' body. Then she wrings her hands as she embraces Jesus' feet (ACE 4 332-340).

Magdalen, Salome, Mary Cleophas, and Johanna Chusa go to the city to purchase more herbs, flowers, and spices to take to the tomb the next morning. Salome, a wealthy relative of Joseph, shares the expense of the items with Magdalen. Very early in the morning, the holy women head to the gate carrying the things purchased. The lanterns of the temple guards frighten the women, and two wait outside the gate. Magdalen has no fear and enters the garden (Salome follows shortly). Magdalen sees the stone rolled off to the right, and, stooping down to look into the burial cave, she sees the burial clothes are empty except for the herbs, etc. She then rushes to tell the disciples and tells Salome as she meets her coming to the tomb. Salome rushes to tell the women. They come and see Cassius who tells them to see for themselves. They enter into the sepulcher and see the angels who tell them Jesus has arisen. They, too, rush to tell the Apostles.

Meanwhile Magdalen awakens John and Peter and tells them the tomb is empty. She rushes back and sees the angels, goes out to see where Jesus has been taken and hears, "Why weepest thou?" Thinking it is the gardener whose dim outline she sees, she asks if he knows where they have taken her Lord. Then she hears, "Mary." Recognizing the voice of Jesus, she cries, "Rabboni" meaning Master and falls on her knees wanting to embrace Jesus' feet. He tells her he has not yet ascended to the Father and not to touch Him. She rushes back to the disciples. The holy women come into the tomb area, They see the apparition of Jesus who says, "All hail" and vanishes. They rush to tell the disciples. John and Peter reach the tomb and see the empty grave clothes. They go back to tell the others. Until John and Peter return to the disciples and Apostles, they do not give credence to the women's reports but consider the whole affair to be just women's imagination (ACE 4 367-373).

Now Magdalen gives no thought of danger as she is overwhelmed with love and sorrow. She goes swiftly through the streets, hair flying. When she finds listeners, she either accuses them of being murderers of Jesus and tells of all the horrors visited upon Jesus or proclaims His resurrection. She wanders through the gardens and talks to the flowers and trees if there are no people to listen. Crowds sometimes gather in sympathy and sometimes to insult her because of her past reputation. Some Jews want to seize her, but she escapes them and continues as before, thinking of nothing but Jesus (ACE 4 389).

The Apostles, now including Thomas, gather in the Supper Room in Jerusalem at the close of the Sabbath, all clothed in long white robes. Mary and Magdalen enter, and the doors close. Other women wait outside the doors. The Apostles pray and sing Psalms. Suddenly, the door to the room opens by itself and Jesus, clothed in light and a white robe passes through the disciples and holy women in the outer hall and enters the room which fills with light. The Apostles all fall back and make way as Jesus says, "Peace be to you!" After speaking to Peter and John regarding some errors they made while attempting healings that had failed, He grasps Thomas' right hand and holds the tip of a finger in the wound of His left hand and then the right. He then directs Thomas' fingers beneath His mantle to the wound in His sides while speaking some words to Thomas. As Thomas then declares, "My Lord, and my God!" he sinks as one unconscious while Jesus holds his hand. While Apostles support Thomas, Jesus pulls him up with His hand. All are greatly moved by this scene. Magdalen is not as emotional as the disciples but appears agitated. Jesus asks for something to eat, blesses the food and shares it.

John carries in from the Holy of Holies a beautiful mantle with red and white stripes and embroidered symbols, which the holy women made during those last days. After a touching and meaningful ceremony, Jesus gives the kneeling Peter a shining morsel, invests him with leadership, and places the mantle made by the women upon him. Peter then rises and speaks to the assembly with new dignity. While Peter speaks, Jesus disappears without addressing either His mother or Magdalen (ACE 4 395–398).

Jesus appears to the five hundred gathered with the Apostles, disciples, and all the holy women on an elevated hill. Peter and the other Apostles are speaking to the crowd about the events of the Passion, resurrection, appearances of the Lord, and their obligations as followers. Jesus appears and walks near the holy women who kneel before Him as He speaks to them. He continues to the pillar where Peter stands and takes his place. He then speaks to the 500 and tells them of the hardships of following Him, leaving relatives behind and facing persecution. About 200 then leave. Jesus then speaks more gravely about the suffering and persecution to come but also mentions receiving eternal rewards. He gives specific directions to the Apostles and disciples. Then He vanishes (ACE 4 408–9).

Later, we see in Bethany, the Apostles gather with about 300 of the faithful, including fifty women. They have given all to the Community (the forming church). Martha and Magdalen are hosting the Blessed Virgin, who has come from Jerusalem. All gather in the open hall of Lazarus' court for a love-feast of sharing the bread and cup. Later, many temple guards arrive from Jerusalem and require the Apostles to appear at the Bethany Council House. The Bethany magistrates back the Apostles and tell the officials from Jerusalem that if these men have committed crimes, arrest them but the soldiers are disturbing the peace and must leave. In order to appease the Sanhedrin deputies also present, Peter sends 123 of the faithful to separate houses given over to the Community. The fifty women also go to live in groups. Peter instructs all to return to Bethany before Christ's ascension day (ACE 4 410–412).

There is a great pooling of property among these followers of the Christ. The in pouring of converts from other areas is so great that negotiations have to take place to procure suitable housing or land on which to build. To obtain these needs, the disciples have to release the inn outside Bethany and have no permanent residents in the inn toward Bethlehem outside of Jerusalem. A new complex between Bethany and Bethphage requires many different materials and supplies to start the construction. Magdalen and Martha give up their Bethany dwellings while Lazarus gives all he has (which is considerable) to the Community. Joseph of Arimathea and Nicodemus also give all. When they become priests, Peter puts deacons in their former posts of supervising alms distribution and providing for the Community (ACE 4 418).

Another love-feast occurs in the house of the Last Supper, and, aware that Jesus will very soon be ascending, all want to be with Him as much as possible. Afterwards, all assemble under the trees where Jesus gives a long instruction and His blessing. He gives His hand to His mother as she stands before the holy women. All are quite touched. Emmerich feels that Magdalen very much wants to embrace Jesus' feet, but she does not due to Jesus' grave demeanor that inspires holy fear. They weep when He leaves (ACE 4 423).

Following the ascension of Jesus, the day of Pentecost arrives. Part of the gathering involves baptisms in the Pool of Bethsaida a short distance from the Last Supper house. Those being baptized that day are those whom John baptized. The holy women distribute white baptismal gowns to those being baptized. The holy women also receive baptism. The Community that day adds 3,000 members (ACE 4 434).

Eight days after Pentecost, the Apostles and disciples, after spending the whole night in the house of the Last Supper, go to the temple. The holy women and Blessed Virgin arrive there earlier. Peter delivers a powerful message to a large crowd. The women go to the Last Supper house to kneel and pray alone before the Blessed Sacrament. Magdalen prays for a time in the entrance–hall. Sometimes she stands, sometimes kneels, and at times lies down with arms out stretched (ACE 4 441).

It is about a year after the crucifixion that Stephen is stoned. The Christians disperse as the settlement near Jerusalem dissolves. Some Christians are murdered. Magdalen goes to live in a cave as directed by Jesus. Then Lazarus, Martha, and Magdalen are arrested and exiled over the sea (ACE 4 449, 460).

The Metaphysical Bible Dictionary, under the entries Lazarus, Martha, and Mary, provides interesting and enlightening thoughts about the symbolical meaning of these biblical characters. The entries are quite long but very worthwhile. Under Lazarus' entry, it says,

> Lazarus: Bringing this sleeping life to outer consciousness is no easy task . . . The higher must enter into sympathy and love with the lower to bring about the awakening— "Jesus wept" . . . The "stone" that holds the sleeping life is the tomb of matter in subconsciousness in the belief in the permanency of present material laws. This "stone" must be rolled away through faith. The man who wants the inner life to spring forth must believe in the reality of spiritual powers and must exercise his faith by invoking in prayer the presence of the invisible but omnipresent God.

Martha's entry says,

> Martha represents the outer activity of the soul that is receiving the higher self; Mary represents the inner or soul

receptivity. Martha desires to show her love by service; Mary shows hers by learning at Jesus' feet. Both of these activities are necessary . . . We should not set greater value on active service than on quiet, loving receptivity to the Spirit of truth within us.

And Mary's entry offers,

Mary sits at the feet of Jesus . . . Feet symbolize the understanding, and when Mary pours upon Jesus' feet the precious ointment she is symbolically bathing His understanding with the fragrance of love. This lesson of John 12:1-8 and Matthew 26:6-13 is of great import to metaphysicians.

Chapter 6

Seraphia/Veronica and Johanna Chusa

Seraphia is a holy woman acquainted with the holy family from early childhood. She is one of the twenty-four girls who assist in preparing the feast in Mary's honor when Mary is going into the temple. Seraphia is between ten and twelve years old when she helps prepare garlands and wreaths for Mary and her companions. When the girls are walking to the temple, they pass Seraphia's house, situated between the temple and Mount Calvary (ACE 1 170). Simeon and his son Obed (both associated with the temple) are relatives of Seraphia. Obed receives baptism from John (ACE 3 594). Seraphia is also a relative of John the Baptist as her father is the son of Zachary's brother (ACE 4 256).

When the twelve-year-old Jesus stays behind at the temple, it is Seraphia who takes food to Him. She is older than Mary but not yet married at that time (ACE 4 257).

Seraphia does not marry until later in life. Her husband is Sirach, a descendent of the chaste Susanna of the Bible. He is a council member in the temple and, therefore, opposes her involvement with Jesus and the holy women. To stop these connections, he sometimes confines her to a prison cell for lengthy periods of time. Fortunately, Sirach does not spend much time at home but is away tending to his duties. Even when he is at home, Seraphia seldom sees him. Finally, Nicodemus and Joseph of Arimathea convince Sirach to convert, and he then allows Seraphia to freely follow Jesus. When Caiaphas conducts Jesus' trial, all three of these men resign from the Sanhedrin (ACE 4 257). Seraphia is still a beautiful woman even past fifty, and Joseph of Arimathea is delighted when she tells Sirach that she would prefer to separate from him rather than from Jesus. Thereafter, Sirach condescends to his wife (ACE 4 390). Emmerich compares Seraphia to St. Catherine in manner—both are courageous, straight forward, and resolute. Her maid serves her for years, even after Jesus' death (ACE 3 437).

Seraphia attends the wedding at Cana, coming from Jerusalem with Mary Marcus and Obed. She brings with her a beautiful basket of flowers and a nice assortment of fancy foods (ACE 2 46).

The inn known as the disciples' inn is a house to the north of Mount Calvary on the northwest side of Jerusalem. Seraphia is in charge of this inn. She also supplies items from her house in Jerusalem. The Apostles carry table service of all kinds in baskets to the house owned by Nicodemus.

They even borrow the wonderful chalice from Seraphia which Jesus uses for the Blessed Sacrament. This chalice has quite a long history. Seraphia buys it from the temple. Occasionally, an old item, whose use is no longer known, is made over, melted down, or sold. The material from which the chalice is made is unknown and resists being melted down. Jesus apparently knows all about the chalice and its history. It is shaped like a pear, is quite large, has two handles, has a spoon hidden in the foot, and is brown in color overlaid with gold. The whole set includes small cups around the very large one. The seven churches eventually receive one cup each while the main chalice stays in Jerusalem under the care of James the Less. Emmerich claims that Melchizedek gets it in Semiramis, takes it to Canaan, and uses it to offer bread and wine to Abraham. Then, he gives it to Abraham. It passes on to Noah and to Moses. As the nun looks at the chalice, in her vision, she receives its history. She sees the chalice well preserved and thinks it will reappear some day (ACE 4 545).

The number of children Seraphia has is uncertain. The visions mention an adopted daughter of nine and more than once a son. This son is usually mentioned in regard to Jesus because he later becomes His disciple (ACE 1 347). We learn the name of Seraphia's son in a trip he makes to Bethsaida with Jesus. Three men accompany Him; a relative of Peter, who later becomes a disciple; a son of a widowed relative of Jesus; and Amendor, the son of Seraphia (ACE 1 349). When Jesus is instructing a crowd on a mountain near Thisbe and Adama, Lazarus sends the sons of Seraphia and Johanna Chusa to warn Him that the Pharisees have two spies there to report on Him. Jesus knows who the spies are but does not identify them. He merely tells the crowd that enemies are among them, but that they will not keep Him from fulfilling the mission assigned by His Father (ACE 2 158).

Seraphia is present when Jesus announces the death of John, the Baptist. This occurs after John's arrest and imprisonment brought about after Salome dances for Herod. He is so pleased with her voluptuous dance, that he offers her anything she wants—up to one-half of his kingdom. Salome's mother tells her to ask for John's head.

Herod's guards behead John in his cell. Salome receives John's severed head and carries it to the kitchen, where her mother eagerly waits. Herodias lifts the cover from the head and shouts insults at John. She takes a skewer and jams it into the tongue, cheeks, and eyes. Finally, she kicks the head into a pit, and it ends up with the garbage in the sewer. Both Jesus and Mary are aware of this hideous deed. It is in Juttah, John's birthplace, where Jesus finally announces John's death to the disciples, the holy women present (Mother Mary, Mary Marcus, Johanna Chusa, Susanna, Seraphia), and relatives of John (ACE 4 164).

The women have come to Juttah ahead of the men, and Mary tells of her visit to Elizabeth before John and Jesus are born. It is a very sad gathering, where Jesus discloses John' beheading; that the body lies untouched, and that the head, thrown into a sewer, will be retrieved (ACE 4 174). Emmerich describes the recovery of the body from the prison cell by the disciples, aided by the prison guards. She describes a bright light filling the cell and of the apparition of a tall lady, Elizabeth, John's mother, who aids, unseen by the disciples. The deserting guards and the disciples transport the body to Juttah, where many Essenes and relatives lament not being able to see John's head (ACE 3 179–187).

With the knowledge of the resting place of John's head, Johanna Chusa and Seraphia with one of the relatives set out for Machaerus. Some of Herodias' servants tell them the location, but they cannot open and drain the vaulted sewer to rescue the severed head. Some time later, the sewers are drained for maintenance. A group of women from Juttah and Jerusalem gather nearby, praying and fasting. When the workmen leave to eat, the men paid to help the women take them into the sewer. They see other heads besides John's in the sewer. Two shafts of light shine on one head, and they see that one belongs to John, which they wrap in linen cloths and take away. The whole project is not without danger. On the roadway they find an unconscious soldier. They lay John's head on the soldier's chest, and he is healed immediately. At last, the head is entombed with the body (ACE 3 58–61).

Jesus spends time with John Mark and Obed at Lazarus' estate near Thirza where He teaches in the synagogue and distributes food to the many poor people in that little place. The people honor both Lazarus and Jesus there. They continue traveling and talking with shepherds and local people until they reach Lazarus' Bethany house. Martha leaves the next morning for Jerusalem to tell Mary Marcus and other holy women that Jesus is coming to Mary Marcus' house. At the dinner that evening, besides Jesus and Lazarus, are Seraphia, Johanna Chusa, Susanna, and disciples of both Jesus and John, John Mark, Simeon's son, Veronica's son, and Aram and Themen (nephews of Joseph of Arimathea).

Jesus and Lazarus return to Bethany, and the next day they attend an entertainment at the public-house owned by Simon. The same group that attended the dinner in Jerusalem is present, including Seraphia. Nicodemus and Joseph of Arimathea attend, and Nicodemus listens to the words of Jesus with astonishment, for he is not yet a follower— much the same as the wavering Simon (ACE 2 107–109).

On another occasion, Jesus visits an area to which Jairus invites Him. Jairus is a married Essenian with a wife and several children. One is a daughter whom Jesus cures of a disease previously. This is not the Jairus of the Gospel. Jesus teaches there, speaking of John's baptism, explaining that it is a preparatory penance baptism, and also telling them of the coming of God's Kingdom. Then, Jesus and the disciples head on towards Bethany. The disciples go to their homes, and only Aram and Themen, nephews of Joseph of Arimathea, go on to Bethany. These nephews, from Joseph's mother's side, are first disciples of John but now follow Jesus. Lazarus comes out to meet Jesus. Many from Jerusalem await Jesus and the nephews. Some holy women including Seraphia are in the group, and Jesus has a private talk with them (ACE 1 483).

Jesus has a special room at Lazarus' house in Bethany and frequently stays there. It is the family oratory and is arranged in the manner of a synagogue with a desk in the center of the room, supplied with rolls of Scripture and prayers. A small room at the side serves as the bedroom (ACE 2 105).

Lazarus, Jesus and five disciples go from Capernaum, but the disciples go on ahead by one road while Jesus and Lazarus move along the less traveled paths. Lazarus later goes on ahead to allow Jesus time alone.

A sizeable group waits in the subterranean vault of the castle for Jesus' arrival. The disciples from Jerusalem and Lazarus are there, as well as more disciples and followers of Jesus. The holy women present include Seraphia, Johanna Chusa, Mary Maroni, the widow of Obed, Martha, and her old servant, now a holy woman, too. Among the men are Nicodemus, Joseph and his nephews, and the sons of Simeon, Obed, Johanna Chusa, and Seraphia, Nicodemus eagerly listens to Jesus' words. The men talk with regret about John's arrest and imprisonment. The women sit on cushions at one side of the table (ACE 2 170).

Seraphia and Johanna Chusa are also present at Maroni's house in Naim, when Jesus, after returning from Cyprus, asks them about events in Jerusalem during His absence. The women give animated reports, and Jesus reprimands them for making judgments (ACE 3 436). Emmerich next sees Seraphia with Mary Marcus and about a dozen men in Nicodemus' house in Jerusalem, including John and Matthew. Jesus is instructing (ACE 3 486). This is not long after Lazarus comes forth from the tomb.

On Palm Sunday a procession is moving through Jerusalem, waving palm branches. Many come out of the city to meet Jesus, the Apostles, and disciples. The High Priest rounds up the husbands and relatives whose wives and children run out to meet Jesus. These people are taken to the great court and kept there. Apparently Seraphia, who has two children with her, is in the group running out of the city. She spreads her veil in the path and then does the same with the veil of one of the children with her. She retrieves the veils after Jesus passes and joins the holy women at the end of the procession, about seventeen women.

Following the happy procession, Jesus teaches in the women's section of the temple and at Lazarus'. He tells plainly what is going to transpire; people do not understand but are upset. When He leaves the temple, He says that He will never enter it again in the body. He goes to Lazarus' and instructs during the evening meal. The women serve it because they no longer stay as separate as previously. Many people are greatly upset by Jesus' predictions as the disciples repeat them. Emmerich sees Seraphia in her house, wringing her hands and lamenting. Even her husband inquires about her distress (ACE 4 48).

Anna and Caiaphas lay their plans and reach out to all who hate Jesus. Emmerich gives a long list of reasons these sinful and evil people wish Jesus harm. The disciples and Apostles, for the most part, wander in the valleys around Jerusalem or hide at Mount Olivet in the caves (ACE 4 137). Malicious speeches fill the air. Many criticize the women who follow Jesus. They blast Lazarus and his sisters, John Mark's mother, and Johanna Chusa, and they relish the thought of Seraphia being humbled before her husband, who wanted her to have nothing to do with that Galilean (ACE 4 135–137).

When Jesus appears before Pilate, the various Jewish sect members cry out that they will be defiled if they go into the judgment hall. A man then declares in this nature, "Yes, that hall has been consecrated by blood of innocents. Jesus, only, of the Jews is pure and innocent." This man is Zadock, a wealthy cousin of Seraphia's husband who lost two little boys to Herod's slaughter of the innocents in this very court. After that loss, he withdrew and lived with his wife in continency like an Essenian. Once, at Lazarus' house, he listened to Jesus speak (ACE 4 185).

The battered, bloody Jesus is struggling with the cross. Seraphia watches for the procession, which will come near her house. She has a little adopted girl by the hand as they come rushing out of the house. Seraphia is veiled and has a piece of linen cloth over her shoulder. The little girl is about nine and holds beneath her mantle the expensive, spiced wine Seraphia hopes to give to Jesus to drink. Seraphia pushes through the crowd with the child clinging to her clothes and kneels before Jesus, saying she wants to wipe the Lord's face. Jesus takes the veil and presses it to His face, then returns it with thanks to Seraphia. The child shyly offers the wine toward Jesus, but the soldiers stop her. The mounted Pharisees and executioners are furious and beat and yank Jesus while Seraphia and the child rush back to the house. Seraphia spreads the veil on the table (the same veil she spread before Jesus on Palm Sunday) and faints. The little girl weeps beside her. A friend enters and sees the woolen veil with the bloody imprint of Jesus' face. She rouses Seraphia to show her the imprint. It is customary to offer this type veil to someone in sorrow to wipe away tears as a gesture of sympathy. This memento hangs at the head of Seraphia's bed until her death when it passes by the holy women to Jesus' mother, then to the Apostles, and, finally, to the church. Because of this action, Seraphia is ever after called Veronica, which means "true image." (ACE 4 254–256).

The holy women come to Veronica's house and marvel at the image of Jesus. They take the wine, and at the place of execution pay a man to take the wine to the executioners to give to Jesus. The soldiers drink it themselves and offer Jesus a drink from one of two jugs nearby. One contains vinegar with gall, and the other holds wine mixed with myrrh and wormwood. Jesus tastes the drink offered but does not drink (ACE 4 268). At the crucifixion, Veronica and Johanna Chusa sit back in the second group, a little distance from the cross with seven other holy women. Veronica helps with the cleansing of Jesus' body for burial and follows close behind the litter carrying His body to His tomb (ACE 4 330, 339).

Three years after the Ascension of Christ, officials in Rome seek proof of Jesus' death and resurrection. An official takes Nicodemus, Seraphia, and a disciple related to Johanna Chusa to Rome. Emmerich sees Veronica with the sick Emperor showing him two cloths. One is the veil with Jesus' facial impression. The other has the impression of Jesus' battered body—possibly one of the cloths used for washing His body. Without touching either cloth, or being moved by them, the Emperor is, nevertheless, healed. He then offers Veronica a home with servants as a reward. She desires to return to Jerusalem to die where Jesus lived. When the persecutions begin, after the exile of Lazarus and his sisters, Veronica flees. She is captured and imprisoned. She dies of starvation (ACE 4 258). Emmerich sees a daughter of Veronica present at the death of Mary. Along with Mary Marcus, she helps to prepare Mary's body for burial (ACE 4 467).

Johanna Chusa is one of the very few holy women mentioned in the New Testament. In Luke 8:1-3 we read, "And it came to pass after these things Jesus was traveling in cities and villages, preaching and giving good news of the kingdom of God And his twelve were with him. And the women who were healed of diseases and unclean spirits, Mary who is called of Magdala, from whom seven demons went out, and Joanna, the wife of Chusa and many others, who ministered to them of their wealth." The nun describes Johanna as an energetic, tall, somewhat pale woman with a rather serious manner (ACE 3 436). When Johanna is in Mary's house outside of Nazareth, the nun indicates that Johanna is a relative of Anna the prophetess (ACE 1 366). Another relative hosts Joseph, Mary, and the baby Jesus when they present Jesus at the temple. They stay two nights with an elderly couple, married Essenians, who live fairly close to the temple. They have an inn for poor people, and Jesus and the disciples frequently stay there on their travels. The wife is a relative of Johanna Chusa. Another relative of Johanna comes from Jerusalem with Obed, Simeon's son; and a relative of Veronica to meet Jesus at the disciples' inn near Bethany. This relative later becomes Bishop of Kedar. At one time, he lived a hermit's life near the date trees that bent down to allow Mary to pick their fruit when the holy family was fleeing to Egypt (ACE 3 594). The disciple, Epaphras, is a servant and messenger to the priests in the temple, before performing similar duties with the disciples. He, too, is a relative of Johanna, and the Emperor's official takes him along with Nicodemus and Veronica back to Rome (ACE 4 258).

In at least one instance, Jesus accepts hospitality at Johanna Chusa's house in Jerusalem. The next morning, He goes with some disciples to the Pool of Bethsaida for the purpose of curing pitiful invalids who are more or less abandoned in a closed room. One cured person is a man paralyzed for thirty-eight years. The disciples bring bread, clothes, and other items furnished by the holy women and distribute them among these poor people. The disciples, too, cure people, all of whom are told to go wash in the pool and go quietly to their homes (ACE 3 189).

Jesus and four of the holy women head to Bethany from different places and paths. In addition to the Virgin Mary, the four holy women are Johanna Chusa, Mary Cleophas, Mary Salome, and the widow Lea. They walk single file on narrow paths. Jesus arrives at Lazarus' house, ahead of the women. The nun sees them staying at an inn between the two deserts of Gibea and Ephraim, nearly five hours from Bethany. There are two apartments under a shed with light walls. The front space has two rows of alcoves where the women sleep. The back space is a kitchen. Apparently, male servants accompany the women, and they sleep in an open hut where a fire burns. The next morning, the women continue toward Bethany and arrive well after noon. Martha, Veronica, Mary Marcus, and Susanna greet them. They give the arrivals the necessary items for foot washing, a place to change clothing, and then refreshments. After these actions, Jesus and the men come from Lazarus' house to Martha's house to greet these additional holy women. Jesus takes His mother aside to talk privately and to tell her of his coming fast in the desert. That evening all attend a feast at Lazarus' house. The women eat separately (ACE 1 394, 401, 405).

Shortly after Jesus returns from his fast in the desert, He travels with Andrew and some disciples. At Silo, the others head on to Galilee while Jesus and some of John's disciples travel to Kibzaim, a Levitical city. He stays with the man who heads the school there. Lazarus, Martha, Johanna Chusa, the son of Simeon, and Lazarus' old servant arrive to salute Jesus. This group is on the way to Cana to the wedding. Jesus continues on His mission before turning to Cana. The women and Lazarus meet Mother Mary at Capernaum. They then go to meet Jesus at Tiberias. Simeon's son and the bridegroom, Nathanael—son of Seba,

Sofe's daughter (Anna's sister), who does not live in Cana but is married there—travels with the group (ACE 2 32, 34).

Johanna has a son, but his name is not given. He is mentioned along with Veronica's son when Lazarus sends them to seek Jesus on a mountain near Thisbe and Adama to warn Him that two spies are among the crowd there (ACE 2 158). On another occasion, two Egyptian disciples and Johanna's son meet Jesus, Peter, and John south of Samaria (ACE 3 143).

It is Johanna Chusa and Veronica who seek to find John's head in the sewer. They are unable to find it until two months later when the sewer is drained for cleaning. It is not clear whether they are actually present at that time to help. The group of women and their servants who succeed in finding the head are from both Juttah and Jerusalem. Once they rescue the head in the second attempt and leave for Juttah, they go only a short distance when they see about a thousand of Herod's soldiers heading toward the castle. They manage to hide in a cave. They then continue through the mountains and come upon the unconscious, wounded soldier. They place John's head on his chest, and he is healed. The soldier remarks that while unconscious, he sees John, and John helps him. They do not tell him about the head. The group takes the head to near Hebron and gives it to the Essenians. Some receive healing when they touch John's head. The Essenians wash the head, anoint it with ointments, and solemnly place it with the body (ACE 3 187–188).

By this point, Johanna is a widow. She serves as Martha's primary assistant during the Passion of the Lord and the scattering of the disciples (ACE 4 360, 365, 390).

At the crucifixion, Johanna is with the holy women in the second group from the cross. Afterward, she, too, follows behind the litter carrying Jesus' body to the tomb. She goes with three other holy women to purchase spices, ointments, and herbs for the embalming, which they take to the tomb the next morning.

Chapter 7

The Transformation of Three Adulteresses into Holy Women

*T*here are three holy women, in particular, who dramatically demonstrate the transforming power of Jesus the Christ. One is Mercuria, the pagan priestess; another is Dina, the Samaritan; and the third is Mary the Suphanite. All are from different areas and different circumstances. Dina and Mary become friends, but it is unlikely either ever meets Mercuria.

Jesus and some disciples, including one new one named Jonas, travel to Cyprus, an island near Turkey at the eastern edge of the Mediterranean Sea. He is well received in Salamis, where pagans and Jews of no specific sect live together but on different streets. Jesus teaches in the synagogue where the Jews hear Him interpret the Scriptures in a most enlightening manner. He teaches the pagans in a school, and they treat Him with respect. Jonas takes Jesus and the disciples to his father's large farmhouse surrounded by gardens. The father is an Essenian. Living with him in a separate part of the house are several widowed relatives, nieces, and daughters. He invites Jesus and His followers to come the next day for a meal (ACE 3 34).

Jesus and the disciples are busy preparing an appropriate place for baptism, and many people receive baptism. The Roman Commandant wants to meet this new teacher and sends an invitation for Him to come to his house. Jesus accepts and sees the Commandant sitting on the balcony dressed in a military costume with soldiers standing behind him. The pagans are amazed at the respect their leader, who respects Jewish Law, shows Jesus. He has many questions for Jesus. Servants serve refreshments to Jesus and the disciples, and the Commandant is eager to hear more (ACE 3 345).

From a window, a pagan woman observes Jesus talking with the Commandant (with whom she is intimately involved). She sees a halo of light around Jesus' head, which causes such intense emotions of love to rise in her that she faints. As she regains consciousness, she sees her life pass before her, and what she sees frightens her. She makes inquiries about Jesus and, from some Jewish women, learns of His healing of Magdalen and also about Enue, the woman cured of the issue of blood. She sends a messenger to the inn where Jesus is staying and asks that He go with her to a garden to speak with a woman in distress. He and the disciples go to the place. The woman they meet there is Mercuria— a woman deeply involved in paganism and its abhorrent practices. She is married and has three children, two little girls and an older boy, who is not the son of her husband (unknown to him). She is a tall woman dressed in a long white mantle of a soft clinging material that clearly outlines her figure. She refers to Magdalen and Enue and Jesus having healed them. She wants healing, too, but tells Jesus that, since she's not physically sick, maybe he cannot heal her ((ACE 3 357).

Jesus speaks to her in a merciful manner. He tells her to keep God's commandments and not to commit adultery. She really does not comprehend Jesus or His power. He continues telling her to give up her decadent life which he details to her and urges her to denounce paganism and its debauchery. She is very upset and weeps as she returns to her home. In her apartments, she paces up and down, wringing her hands, wrapping her mantle about herself, and throwing herself in a corner. Her rather slow husband and her maids fear she has lost her mind. She is filled with remorse for her many sins. All she can think of is going to Palestine and joining the holy women.

The house in which Mercuria lives eventually becomes the home of St. Catherine. There Catherine's father, Costa, receives large possessions and marries a daughter of the pagan priestly family of Mercuria. Catherine despises the idols and puts them out of sight Her father confines her for this. The temple of Mercuria's pagan religion has a huge statue of a goddess shining like gold with the body of a fish and the head of a horned cow. Sacrifices to this goddess include children, especially crippled children, and Mercuria is a priestess in this temple (ACE 3 364).

Jesus and the disciples convert 570 souls of pagans and Jews in Cyprus. They travel over the area converting many. Jesus spends much time bringing together husbands, wives, and children who suffer because of adultery. He speaks separately with the adults, and allows them to confess their sins, which include children conceived outside of marriage. Then, he brings the husband, wife, and children together and listens to them recommit themselves to each other and the care and love of the children. Before he leaves Cyprus, he returns to Salamis (ACE 3 370).

Mercuria requests an interview with Jesus. She takes her two sweetly dressed daughters with her. Jesus speaks long and earnestly with her, and she weeps bitterly that she must leave her son, her pagan parents, and little sister behind. Jesus consoles her and assures her of pardon. The little girls cry and cling to their mother. Many Cypriots go to Palestine by boat. Mercuria brings considerable wealth with her, becomes one of the holy women, and contributes greatly to the building of the Christian settlement between Ophel and Bethany. At first, the Cypriots live in caves until the buildings are ready. At the time of the stoning of Stephen, the settlement is attacked and destroyed, and Mercuria loses her life (ACE 3 427).

The story of the Samaritan woman talking with Jesus at the well is in John 4:7. The nun describes the setting of this story as the land of Joseph's inheritance—known also as Jacob's well. Andrew, James the Greater, and Saturnin go to Sichar to buy food. Jesus sits by the well waiting for someone to come open the well. A pretty Samaritan woman of about thirty appears carrying a bottle made of leather. The woman is rather ornately dressed and carries a large camel hair apron to put on and protect her dress when necessary. She comes on the winding path and cannot see Jesus until she is right in front of Him. She lowers her veil and stops because Jesus is right in her path. Jesus greets her and tells her He needs a drink of water. She questions Him about being there alone, and He tells her the others are in Sichar to obtain food. Dina says she passed them on the way to the well. She then proceeds to unlock the door to the spring house. They have further conversation about a Jew asking something of a Samaritan and the living water concept comments made by Jesus. Next, Jesus tells her to bring her husband to the well. Dina says she has no husband. He replies to her symbolically, saying the Samaritans have espoused the idols of five nations and are not married to God. They continue in this vein, and she understands what He means. She feels He is giving her the living water and rushes to spread the word to the other Samaritans and the man who lives with her (ACE 2 180).

During Jesus' conversation with Dina, Andrew, James, and Saturnin are observing and disapproving of Jesus and Dina talking. They do not understand why He doesn't eat the food but instead leaves with them toward Sichar. Dina reaches Sichar and very excitedly tells the people to come to the well to see the man who has told her all her life secrets and is certainly the Christ. Jesus and the three others meet Dina coming back. She turns and walks to Sichar with them. Jesus talks much to her and truly tells her all the facts of her life. She promises that she and her husband will abandon all and follow Jesus.

Dina is an intelligent woman whose Jewish mother and pagan father died when she was young. Her nurse was an evil influence. By her five husbands, she bore three daughters, and two sons, but all the children remain with their fathers. However, the two sons do become disciples of Jesus. When Dina leaves Damascus, she comes with her present husband, who is a relative of a former husband (a rich merchant).

They come to Sichar because she follows the Samaritan religion. The nun observes that there are things in the lives of Dina and Magdalen that are similar but that Dina has fallen farther than Magdalen.

Jesus, the Apostles, and disciples—now including Peter and the others returning to Jesus from assignments—go into Sichar to a large, receptive crowd. Jesus speaks kindly and graciously to them and tells them to believe what Dina relates to them. They want Jesus to stay and teach them. He promises them He will return soon (ACE 2 180–191).

Some of the disciples continue with Jesus to the shepherds' huts. In the largest hut, Mother Mary, Mary Cleophas, James the Greater's wife, and two widows await Him. They spend the whole day waiting with food and bottles of balsam. Jesus takes His mother's hands in His in greeting her. They eat a meal then under a tree.

After Jesus heals a lame child at His mother's request, several people from Sichar, including Dina, arrive but hold back. Dina finally moves forward and talks with the women. Then, the women and Mother Mary leave for Galilee. Jesus returns to Sichar with Dina and the other Samaritans (ACE 2 192).

The Samaritans receive Jesus joyfully in Sichar. Dina gains special recognition for finding Jesus. The people are greatly touched to be treated so kindly by Jesus, a Jew. They agree with Dina, "He is the Messiah!" They want to know where to receive baptism since John is in prison. Jesus says John's disciples are baptizing across the Jordan in Ennon. Dina and her companions decide to part ways. Jesus advises them, and they consecrate their wealth to the poor and the future Church (ACE 2 195).

Other Samaritans who benefit from Jesus' visit to Sichar and surrounding areas appear in the Cayce readings. Although none are labeled holy women, they illustrate the great benefit gained due to Dina and Jesus meeting at the well. One such person seems to be the woman at the well (451-2).

> In the one then before this we find during that period when the Master walked in the earth, and this entity that one to whom the Master spoke at the well in the way, and a sister then of those that later become messengers and understanders of that being taught. The entity lost and gained, through this experience; for as the entity widened its influence for that which brought those of distorted emotions and ideas in the minds of individuals during that period, so

with the awakening of the water of life springing anew in the hearts and souls of those that made Him as the ideal, did the entity bring into the minds, hearts, and souls of those first of its own household, then of the multitudes, then of the greater masses, that of the *Beauty of life* in Him, of the glories of the Father in Him, as may be manifested in the lives of individuals who have Him as their ideals, whether pertaining to the secular things of life or otherwise—for the crust of bread glorified by Him feeds in the physical body those things that bring glories in the hearts and minds of individuals, where the sumptuous board of those that wander far away must bring dimness of eye, solemnness of feeling, want and desire in the hearts of those that follow such; but keeping in that way and that understanding as gained then, as Jodie in this experience, may the entity throughout this present experience make for that way that will give understanding to the many.

Whether Jodie is the name of the person as the Samaritan woman or the woman who receives the reading is unclear, but most likely Jodie is the name of the recipient of the reading.

In another reading a forty–seven–year–old woman (428-4) learns she as Josie is a sister of the Samaritan woman and is among those who go to the well to hear the truths presented. She gives much to others and is one "who is sent to the lost sheep of the house of Israel." Also, Josie is an aid for understanding to those she contacts. She is in the household of a ruler. In a subsequent reading (428-5) "the ruler is named Pagosius [?] as *of* the kingdom of those of Syria *to whom* Samaria had paid tribute." Josie helps establish a "church that later was ministered to by many of those who were His Apostles and teachers; and particularly by Philip, Stephen, Peter, Paul, Apollos. Later, in the latter portion of the entity's experience, the entity was the *mother*, as it were, of the church—known as Pisillia [?] [Pisidia?] . . . "

In a separate reading, Cayce tells another woman she is a sister to the Samaritan at the well (2112-1), has the name Selma at that time, and works at sharing the good news to residents of Mount Seir. Phoebe

(379-3) learns of Jesus through the Samaritan woman's message. She becomes a wanderer in order to hear Jesus teach and a singer and dancer to provide the money to follow Him. As the persecutions begin in the city, she works with Andrew, Bartholomew, and Jude to bring messages of help to the despairing of body, mind, or spirit.

One last active Samaritan due to Jesus being at Jacob's well is Jeaniel (1552-1). She is a young woman much impressed by Jesus. She is in the crowd when Jesus enters Jerusalem triumphantly and makes close associations with church leaders in many lands. She is helpful to those at Bethany—Mother Mary, Magdalen, and Martha and is also helpful later with Lucius, John, Luke, and Mark.

Jesus continues His ministry of instructing and healing. He sends Monahem, a formerly blind man now healed by Jesus, to take a message to Lazarus. Lazarus comes back from Bethany with Joseph's two nephews, and Jesus meets with them. By these men, the holy women send a variety of gifts and money to Jesus. Some of this comes from Dina, who visits the holy women at Capernaum where she contributes much money. Veronica and Johanna Chusa also visit Mary, and they go to see Magdalen to lift her depressed spirits. They take Dina to Bethany with them, and here an unnamed elderly, wealthy widow joins Martha's group and gives all she owns to the beginning community (ACE 2 429).

The nun compares Magdalen and Dina after they attend Jesus' instruction at Gabara. She believes Magdalen to be more beautiful and taller than Dina. However Dina is active, cheerful, supple, humble, affectionate, and ready to help. But compared to the Virgin Mary, they both fall short (ACE 2 483). During a meal they are serving Jesus, the Pharisees in Betheron reproach Him about a number of faults they see. One charge is that He allows women with bad reputations to follow Him. They know about the conversions of Magdalen, Mary Suphan, and the Samaritan. He responds to them that if they knew Him, they would understand that He pities sinners. Then He relates a parable to them to illustrate His point, but they do not connect with the application (ACE 3 159).

The holy women gather at the inn at the foot of the mountain where Jesus is speaking to a multitude on that mountain near Gabara. They are preparing for the needs of Jesus and the disciples. It is a long day for Jesus, and he speaks without an intermission until His voice becomes shrill. Finally, He comes down to the inn. In addition to those holy women, who arrive early, others there include Martha, Dina, Mary Suphan, Maroni of Naim, Mother Mary, and their escort Lazarus. Also, the Galilean women bring many provisions, material, and clothing. They have a meal ready for Jesus and the disciples (ACE 3 318–320).

At the time of the crucifixion of Christ, Dina the Samaritan is not in the burial procession but is instead in Bethany with Martha and Lazarus, Mary Suphan, and Maroni of Naim. This group later goes to Jerusalem to observe the Sabbath. They arrive after dark and join the groups of Apostles, disciples, and holy women gathered together in deep mourning and relating again their sorrowful experiences (ACE 4 243).

Mary of Suphan meets Jesus at Ennon. He goes to Ennon and finds a large crowd awaiting Him. He heals many people on the way and more upon arriving in Ennon. A middle-aged woman, quite beautiful and ornately dressed, tries to approach Jesus. She is anxious, red–eyed from weeping, timid and ashamed, and cannot find a way through the crowd filling the court. About ten Pharisees are keeping order. When they see the woman, they go to her, and she begs them to take her to the prophet so that He will forgive her sins and cure her. The Pharisees immediately tell her to go home that the prophet will have nothing to do with an adulteress. The woman turns pale, assumes a hopeless expression, throws herself on the ground, tears her mantle, jerks off her veil, and wails that the five devils will tear her to pieces, meaning her husband and four lovers. It is quite a spectacle. Some nearby women gather her up and take her home. Jesus is aware of the scene, but He does not want to interfere with the Pharisees who have welcomed Him respectfully. He also knows the woman's time is not yet due. He continues healing and teaching. The teaching ends around three in the afternoon, and the Pharisees and disciples go down the hill to attend an entertainment in a public hall. Near the hall Jesus stops and proclaims a desire to see the woman sent away in the morning. He then goes to her nearby house with two disciples.

Emmerich describes the woman Mary Suphan inside the house be-

ing driven from one corner to another, fully possessed. She sees Jesus
coming, flees to a cellar, and attempts to hide in a huge cask. It bursts
with a loud noise as she attempts to climb into it. Jesus stops, calls her
by name and orders her in the name of God to come to Him. Mary of
Supha crawls to Him on all fours. He orders her to stand up, which she
does, pulling her veil over her face. Jesus orders her to show her face
and then to look at Him. He breathes on her. The nun sees a black vapor
pouring out of Mary in several places, and Mary of Suphan falls unconscious. Her servants are now present after hearing the loud noise of the
breaking cask. Jesus directs them to take their mistress to her bed. Jesus
and the disciples find her bitterly weeping. He places His hand on her
head and announces that her sins are forgiven. She weeps and sits up.
Her three children come into the room: a boy of twelve years and girls
nine and seven. Jesus speaks kindly to the children, asks them some
questions, and instructs them. The children bow at Jesus' feet when
their mother tells them Jesus has cured her. He blesses them, and starting with the boy, has each child place their hands in their mother's
hands. The nun believes Jesus does this to remove the stigma of them
being born to adulterous unions and thus makes them legitimate. Then
Jesus and the disciples go to the entertainment.

Mary is from Supha in the land of Moab. Moab is a descendent of Lot
(Genesis 19:30–38). The Moabites worship a god called Chemash and are
forced to pay tribute to David, partially of Moabite descent. Mary descends from Orpha, the daughter-in-law of Naomi whose other daughter-in-law Ruth went with Naomi to Bethlehem when Naomi's two sons
died, leaving Orpha and Ruth widows. Orpha remarried in Moab, and
Mary descends from that union. She is a rich Jewess and has legitimate
children, but their father has custody of them. Mary moves to Ennon,
does penance for her sins, and behaves so properly that the women
there accept her. While preaching, John the Baptist admonishes Herod
for marrying his brother's wife and this makes a big impact upon Mary,
but she often suffers from demonic possession. Due to her ancestral line
from David, Jesus by grace purifies her to put her back on course (ACE
2 312–319).

Jesus and the disciples go to the entertainment. The Pharisees are not happy about the situation with Mary of Supha, but Jesus treats them with much consideration. About Midway through the evening, Mary's three children enter, nicely dressed, and approach Jesus with crystal vases, containing such things as nard and special, expensive water. They set the presents on the table and kneel before Jesus. Mary and her maids enter with Mary veiled and carrying a large shining vase filled with green foliage and many expensive aromatics. The Pharisees are seething, but Jesus calls Mary to come forward, which she does, and has the children put her present beside theirs on the table. The disapprovers grumble about the waste and giving to the poor instead. Jesus gives the children fruit and treats them and their mother very kindly. He tells the Pharisees that all gifts come from God, and these are gifts of gratitude that also give the people who supply them a livelihood. Mary and the children leave. Jesus offers instruction, focusing on adultery, including spiritual adultery. He compares John's failed attempts to convert Herod, who marries his brother's wife, with Mary's turning from evil of her own accord. Previously, He has already privately consoled Mary in her house, telling her the children will turn out well and suggesting to her that one day she might join the holy women under Martha's supervision (ACE 2 319–320).

Jesus and the disciples travel to other places populated mostly with pagans. They come back from Jogbeha to Ennon and Socath. The people are busy preparing for the feast of tabernacles. They erect a very nice tent, and Mary the Suphanite prepares a solemn reception for Jesus. The important leaders and priests of the city welcome Him, and Mary and her children. After the washing of the feet of Jesus and the disciples, the children present food to the guests. The veiled women bow low to Jesus. Mary invites Jesus and the disciples to her house, and the children joyfully run along side. Jesus acknowledges the little children. Mary tells Him that Dina and the man living with her have come, and he is now baptized. Mary presents Jesus with beautiful, costly robes and a miter, all made by her for the use of the priests. Jesus thanks her graciously and advises her to return to her husband, as the three children in Ennon can be cared for by others. He asks Mary to send a messenger to her husband to come. Then He goes to the baptismal place and instructs the people. Several from Jerusalem appear: Lazarus, Joseph of Arimathea, Veronica, and some disciples. Andrew and John remain for the Sabbath.

For the Sabbath, Jesus teaches in the synagogue on creation, the waters, and man's fall. After the Sabbath, Mary provides entertainment in the public banquet hall. All is beautifully decorated with foliage, flowers, and lamps. Many of the guests are women cured by Jesus. They sit behind a screen to one side. Mary and the children place costly perfumes on the table during the meal, and she pours fragrant balm over Jesus' head. Then she casts herself down before Him. Jesus receives the gifts graciously and relates parables pertinent to the situation. No one criticizes Mary because she is very generous with all and is quite wealthy. Jesus addresses many penitents and focuses on the return of the prodigal son. He then leads the disciples and many inhabitants on a walk outside the city and along the Jordan. All are happy and filled with love. At the end of the Sabbath, a feast of the tabernacles occurs, and the baptized pagans are cordially included by the Jews.

Mary has an interview with Jesus before He leaves Ennon. She is a changed woman, full of love and gratitude, and is busy helping the poor and sick. Jesus tells her a disciple has gone to Bethany to tell the holy women of her conversion. Veronica, Johanna Chusa, and Martha soon thereafter visit Mary. Mary gives rich gifts to Jesus and other people. Jesus immediately has his gifts distributed among the poor (His usual procedure). As he leaves Ennon, people sing songs of praise, present Him with wreaths, and walk a way with Him as He heads to Akrabis (ACE 2 374–387).

When Magdalen arrives at Damna, she parts with Martha and Anna Cleophas to stay in a private apartment where both Dina and Mary Supha visit her. They go to the instruction Jesus gives on the mountain near Gabara. For the most part, the holy women stay at the inn at the foot of the mountain so that Magdalen will not feel uncomfortable with them present. Jesus heals women with blood flow ailments. Then six women well bound, shouting, and creating quite a scene, are pulled along to Jesus by servants. They are terribly possessed, and Mary looks on them with pity, memories, and gratitude as Jesus commands silence of the demons tormenting the women. He has the servants unbind the six women, tells the women to kneel and pray, and lays His hands on them. They momentarily lose consciousness, and Emmerich sees the usual dark vapors issue from the women. Mary, Dina, and Magdalen stay at the inn with the holy women (ACE 2 473–479).

Chapter 8

Mary Marcus, Mother of John Mark

Since Mary Marcus is the mother of John Mark, it will be most help-ful to start with a reading given for the person named as the entity John Mark at the time of Jesus. The reading states:

> As we find, the entity was born during that period which would be known as the sixteenth year of our Lord; his parents were Mary and Marcus, his sisters Rhoda and Mary. He was close to, and a relative of, Chloe and Lois, Josie; all relatives of Mary, the mother of the Lord, of the tribe of Judah; of the household of Marcus; hence sometimes referred to as Marcus, or son of Marcus. In his twelfth year he was healed from an infirmity by the associations with John, the cousin of the Lord, and the Lord. He was one at whose house Peter the apostle came when released from prison, and was a companion . . . with Paul the apostle and Barnabas, and one that returned from the first missionary journey of these two, acting in the capacity of the secretary to Barnabas. He was the first compiler of a letter that later became the gospel known as Mark, collaborating (as

it would be termed in the present) with Peter and Barnabas. He became a helpmeet to many of the early martyrs, suffering martyrdom himself in the latter portion of his experience at that time; being, however, the martyrdom of expulsion and traveling in the latter portion of the experience (after the writings in Rome) to those eastern lands with Andrew, the brother of Peter, who had escaped from those same character of martyrdoms as those that had been sent on to Rome; being sent by Peter *and* by Paul as an emissary to carry the messages of Paul and of Peter to those people whom Andrew was ministering to, rather in what is now called Persia, aiding oft in the *strengthening* of the brethren in the various centers where churches or established organizations had been built by the efforts of Paul, Barnabas, Silas and the other ministers during that period. Oft he was a companion with Luke, who was an associate and companion of Paul oft in his travels. Luke being rather of those peoples that were free (as he was not of the Jewish descent), this aided John Mark in his abilities to go and come rather at ease; hence after becoming more stable (than as a young man) was of so much aid to the peoples during that period.

As yet there are few of the writings or letters of John Mark, or son of Marcus, other than that contained in the gospel known as Mark. This was written during the fifty-ninth year, or during the thirty-fourth year of the entity's experience in that plane.

He assisted Barnabas in the establishing of the church in northern Africa, or Alexandria, where so *much* persecution *later* was shown in the activities in that center. Much that was compiled by the entity in this land was destroyed in or during the second century. This had been compiled in the great library in Alexandria. There are still intact some writings that may yet be reclaimed, in some of the ruins about the place; as well as in some of those cities in Chaldea and Persia where the entity in the last days went in company with Andrew . . .

(Q) Was the whole Gospel of Mark written by him, or was

the last part added on?

(A) The whole Gospel was written rather in collaboration with Peter and Barnabas. This, as given, was the first of the *written* words respecting the acts, the life, the deeds of the Master; while it is shorter in words, there is more in body content of the acts than in most of the other writings. It is nearer in accord with that in Matthew, but not an abridged condition or abridged writing; for Matthew was written from the churches in Pamphylia, while Mark wrote from Rome. There had been some distribution, or a portion had been carried to many of the various groups before Mark's was accepted, and before Matthew's was given; for this was written some ten to eighteen years later.

(Q) Did he associate with the Christ?

(A) As a child.   452-5

The John Mark reading names Mary and Marcus as his parents. Rhoda and Mary are his sisters Mary Marcus also has a maid–servant named Rhoda. The first Rhoda has three daughters and two sons. A daughter of Rhoda, a friend of Mary the Virgin, is one of the three widows, and her two sons are among Jesus' disciples. One of Rhoda's sons marries Maroni, but they have no children. Maroni becomes a widow and marries a relative of her first husband, a nephew of Anna, mother of Virgin Mary, named Eliud. Maroni and Eliud have a son named Martial. To further add to the confusion, twice Mary Marcus is associated with Obed. One reference, which concerns guests at the wedding of Cana, refers to Mary Marcus, Obed, and Veronica coming from Jerusalem (ACE 2 45). Another reference—listing people gathered at Lazarus' house in Bethany—includes the sons of Simeon, Johanna Chusa, Veronica, and Obed. A group of women also listed include Veronica, Johanna Chusa, Susanna, and Mary Marcus, the widow of Obed. It appears that Mark's father dies, and his mother remarries. There are several Mary's and Obed's named that have associations with the relatives and friends of the holy family (ACE 2 171, 455).

Jesus and five of the disciples are visiting near Nazareth. The disciples go to see relatives, and Jesus talks with Eliud the widowed, elderly Essenian much respected by Jesus. This time, there are many at Mary's house including Mary Cleophas, her niece; Johanna Chusa, a cousin of the Prophetess Anna; the Widow Lea; and the relative of Simeon, Mary, mother of John Marc (ACE 1366).

Once, when Jesus arrives at Lazarus' house, Martha goes the next morning to tell Mary Marcus that Jesus and her brother will be arriving at Mary's house in Jerusalem midday. Her house is opposite the Mount of Olives on the outskirts of the city on the eastern side. Dinner is served to Mary Marcus, Jesus, Lazarus, disciples of John and Jesus from Jerusalem, John Marc, Simeon's sons, Veronica's sons, and nephews of Joseph of Arimethea. The women are Veronica, Johanna Chusa, and Susanna (ACE 2 106).

Following the wedding feast in Cana, the holy women attending the wedding, including Jesus' mother stop in with Mary Marcus (ACE 2 114). After the Sabbath, the Pharisees go to Mary Marcus' house hoping to find Jesus and take Him into custody. When they find only the holy women, they harshly order them to leave the city as followers of Jesus.. The frightened and weeping women leave and go to Martha's house in Bethany. Martha is with her sister. Silent Mary is suffering terribly as she sees in the spirit what Jesus must face. She dies in the presence of the holy women who are there because the Pharisees ordered them to leave the house of Mary Marcus. Apparently, Mary Marcus is with these women at Martha's house (ACE 2 121).

Jesus is at Sichor teaching. The two disciples He sends to Capernaum tell Him four disciples are approaching. Jesus walks four hours to meet them and then walks back to Sichor with Peter, Andrew, James the Less, Nathanael Chased, the two disciples serving as messengers, as well as some of the holy women, including Mary Marcus of Jerusalem, and the maternal aunt of the bridegroom Nathanael. (ACE 2 132–133).

On another occasion, Jesus comes with Lazarus and some disciples from the inn at Dothan to meet the holy women coming from Damna. Those named coming with the Blessed Virgin are Mary Marcus, Anna Cleophas, Mary the Suphanite, Johanna Chusa, Veronica, Susanna Alpheus, Dina, Susanna of Jerusalem, and Maroni (ACE 3 125). A short time later some of these women, who include Magdalen, stop in with

Issachar, a sick husband recently healed by Jesus. They do this because the holy women never stay at the public inns. Another group of holy women, whose numbers include Martha and Mary Johanna Marcus, are traveling out in pairs to see about the private inns and supply whatever they need (ACE 3 143).

After the death of John the Baptist, Jesus and His companions gather at John's birthplace in Juttah. Since several of the holy women and disciples from Jerusalem take a shorter route, they arrive ahead of Jesus. He informs them of John's fate. The women present include Mother Mary, Susanna of Jerusalem, Veronica, Johanna Chusa, and Johanna Marcus. The nun refers to Mary Johanna Marcus in different ways. Unless she is just called Mary, it is not difficult to identify her correctly (ACE 3 164).

After Jesus raises Lazarus from the dead, He takes two of the Apostles before daybreak to the house of Nicodemus in Jerusalem. When they reach their destination, Jesus instructs quietly. The nun sees Mary Marcus and Veronica present and at least twelve men. Nicodemus is not there as he is in Bethany to see the risen Lazarus. In Bethany a great, noisy crowd gathers so that Lazarus has to hide, and the Apostles go off from the city in different directions. The nun believes Jesus avoids being stoned by going to Jerusalem (ACE 3 487).

In order to return to Bethany, Jesus takes two relatively new disciples with Him and goes to the disciples' inn outside the city. By night he knocks at Lazarus' gate, and Lazarus admits Him. Holy women await His coming. He later goes to stay at the house of Mary Marcus about fifteen minutes from the temple in Jerusalem. The next day after the Jews leave the temple in Jerusalem, Jesus teaches in the temple where Pharisees are in the crowd. He tells the parable of the wheat field overgrown with weeds requiring careful harvesting of the wheat so as not to uproot it with the weeds (ACE 4 1-3).

When Jesus is preparing for the entrance into Jerusalem, He sends some of the oldest disciples to the house of Mary Marcus. Others He sends to Veronica's house (ACE 4 14).

While Jesus is praying in great anguish in the grotto in the Mount of Olives, a number of the holy women are gathering in the house of Mary

Marcus. Everyone is nervous and anxious that something frightful is about to happen. Magdalen, Mary Cleophas, Mary Salome, Martha, Salome, Mary Marcus, and Jesus' mother decide to go out to learn of any news. They find Lazarus, Nicodemus, Joseph, and some people from Hebron who tell them they have not heard of any immediate danger and comfort the women enough that they return to the house of Mary Marcus (ACE 4 88).

Jesus is under arrest and being painfully escorted to the court, when the nun again sees Mary Marcus in her visions. The disciples disperse as reinforcement soldiers arrive. The holy women, including the Blessed Virgin, Martha, Mary Cleophas, Mary Salome, Susanna, Johanna Chusa, Veronica, Salome, and Mary Marcus along with Lazarus, John Mark, Veronica's son, and Simeon's son head toward the Valley of Josaphat. They soon stop as they get a report from Nathanael who comes from the Apostles in Gethsemane. They wait for the procession to go far enough for them to return to the house of Mary Marcus. After John arrives at the house and answers the anguished Mother's questions, she is escorted to Martha's house, which is near Lazarus' house on the city's west side (ACE 4 126– 130),

Mary Marcus is with the second group of holy women at the crucifixion, and is with that same group following the body of Jesus to the burial site (ACE 4 167, 339). She and some of the other holy women take the elderly sister of Mary, Mary Heli, back to the city from the burial area (ACE 4 342).

John Mark and his mother open their house for the Apostles, disciples, holy women and early Christians in general. For instance, Thaddeus, James the Less, and Eliud go there to see the Virgin Mary and her niece Mary Cleophas (ACE 4 391). Luke attends the love-feast at Lazarus' in Bethany. From there he goes to Jerusalem and stays at the house of John Mark (ACE 4 380). The Virgin Mary obviously likes to stay with Mary Marcus. It is there that she has Veronica and Johanna Chusa, and Mary Marcus accompany her along the Way of Jesus' Passion so that in the twilight, she can walk alone and meditate on the places where Jesus suffers and falls (ACE 4 392–393).

Much later, after the community ownership concept is instituted,

there is mention by the nun of women dwelling together in tents without communication with the men except to receive instruction from the
Apostles. The women work with weaving, embroidery, and tent-mak-
ing among other things. The nun mentions Peter's wife and daughter
among these women, and Mark's wife as well (ACE 4 417). Apparently,
Mary Marcus retains her house.

In Acts 12:12 Peter is released from prison by an angel. He goes to the
house of Mary Marcus, where many of the community are praying. A
little girl named Rhoda answers Peter's knock. Since she is quite young,
it is unlikely she is John Mark's sister.

At the time of Mother Mary's death, the nun reports seeing the holy
women preparing the body for burial. She sees many helping, including John Mark's mother, Mary Marcus (ACE 4 467).

Chapter 9

Susanna, Susana, and Susane

There are at least two holy women named Susanna or Susane. The first person with this name seems to be in the temple at the time Mary enters as a little girl. When the teachers in the temple question Mary, her answers amaze them. Someone recalls the insights of a fifteen-year-old girl from Gophna, noted for her wisdom, named Susanna. Mary seems to be taking her place, and Susanna later joins the holy women (ACE 1 165).

Susanna appears again when Martha has guests at her house in Bethany. Those present include Veronica, Mary Marcus, and a woman described as being from Jerusalem, now aged, but one who left the temple shortly after Mary entered although she desired to stay. God's plans for her included marriage (ACE 1 397). Another reference probably refers to this same Susanna. Jesus instructs people in Luz at the synagogue. Some of His followers have already departed. Lazarus leaves when Jesus finishes teaching. The holy women are already crossing the desert after staying with Susanna in Jerusalem (ACE 1 446). Again, when Jesus leaves Socoth, He goes to an inn in the desert some hours from the Sea of Galilee where He is to meet His mother and some of the holy women. The women decorate the inn for the feast of tabernacles and bring numerous provisions from Gerasa. Several holy women await Jesus including Peter's wife and Susanna of Jerusalem (ACE 1 481). This same Susanna is with a group of women in Jerusalem when Martha comes to tell Mary Marcus that Jesus and Lazarus are coming from Bethany. The other women named as being present for the dinner are Veronica and Johanna Chusa. All live in Jerusalem (ACE 2 107).

Since there are times that Susanna's name appears in a group of holy women in the Emmerich volumes but is not indexed for that page, the indication is that the original compiler of the visions is uncertain as to the correct identity of the Susanna named. Here are a few instances in question that for various reasons I believe Susanna of Jerusalem is the person referenced. When Jesus is in Juttah announcing the death of John to his relatives, a group of people from Jerusalem await His arrival. They include Veronica, Johanna Chusa, Johanna Marcus, and Susanna. It seems logical that the holy women from Jerusalem would travel to-gether (ACE 3 164). The nun speaks of Martha and Susanna being rather general superintendents of the inns looked after by the holy women. She tells of them visiting the inns from Galilee to Samaria and taking supplies loaded on donkeys. This Susanna is listed as one of the holy women headed toward the Valley of Josaphat with the Blessed Virgin (ACE 4 126). A little later the scorners name women who will no doubt regret having followed Jesus and include Susanna among holy women of Jerusalem (ACE 4 135). Finally, at the crucifixion Susanna is one of the second group back from the cross, again with holy women of Jerusalem (ACE 4 267). She is also with that group for the procession to the tomb, and is actually called Susanna of Goghna, temple virgin, in the index.

There is a Cayce reading for a Susanna associated with Martha. It is possible it is the same Susanna appearing in the Emmerich visions. The reading says:

> . . . the entity was in the Promised Land, during those pe-riods when the Master walked in the earth, during those activities in which many came to know Him in His personal activity.

For, the entity then was closely associated and identified with Martha, in the city of Bethany. There the entity was as a helper, as a sister—not in the flesh, but in activity. Thus, through those conditions that arose from the associations, when this became a place for His footsteps, the entity was acquainted with Him. And there the entity learned *patience* There the entity learned the manner in which the spirit of truth, as expressed in the seeds of virtue, of understanding, of acquaintanceship with brotherly love and kindness, may bring into the experience of others those things that make for harmony in the life.

When there were those periods of mourning for the death of the brother of Martha, the entity was among those that mourned.

When there were those preparations for the entertaining, after the resurrection of Lazarus, the entity aided there. And indeed in such preparations, few may be found who may equal the abilities, the virtues of the entity in those directions!

And remember, as He gave, "He that would be the greatest among you will minister to all." These are basic truths, then. Apply them in thy life.

The name then was Susanna, and the entity was among those of the holy women when there were the days of persecution. And there may be read much of the activities of the entity during those periods of trial.   2624-1

Several times the different Susanna's are listed together so that their identities are clear. Jesus heals the man with the withered hand on the Sabbath much to the astonishment and consternation of the Pharisees. Jesus leaves them and goes to Peter's house where He instructs the crowd. His mother appears, accompanied by several holy women including Martha, Dina the Samaritan, Susanna of Jerusalem, and Susanna Alpheus, a daughter of Mary Cleophas and a sister of the Apostles Simon, James, and Thaddeus. She is around thirty years old and has children nearly grown. She joins the holy women in Nazareth where her husband lives. Also she goes by the name of Susanna Cleophas and desires to be of help to the women serving Jesus and His disciples (ACE 3 74).

On one occasion, Jesus visits a girl whom He restores twice. She is a member of Jairus' family, and, after Jesus restores her, the family completely changes and become sincere followers of Jesus. He meets with them and then goes to visit His mother. Stopping with the Blessed Virgin are Susanna Alpheus, Mary Cleophas, Susanna of Jerusalem, Dina the Samaritan, and Martha (ACE 3 94).

Two Cayce readings refer to Susane, child of Cleopas. Although the name spellings are different, the information indicates the two sources concern the same holy woman:

> The entity was in the Palestine land, during that period when the Master walked in the earth, during those periods when there were great understandings and great turmoils about those especially of the city of Bethany when Lazarus was raised from the grave; when those of the followers, those of the sisters—Martha, Mary—made preparation for the supper, after the resurrection or the bringing to life of the brother.
>
> The entity then as a neighbor child, and as a child of Cleopas, in the name Susane, saw those activities, saw also the fears created by those in authority who questioned the child and the parents and those about the feast.
>
> Also the entity heard the words of the teacher, the Master, and these especially then as indicated come to mean a great deal to the entity. Also if the entity is questioned, if there is given to the entity the experiences of the childhood of those nigh unto Him, it will be able to depict in its own, not imagination but in its own experience by turning into the mirror of life and seeing those forces, those experiences that were had by them. As an experience, ask "What do you suppose was served at that supper?" And find *how* many things that are not known in the men of today will be recalled by the entity!
>
> In those things then keep the balance for the entity that they do not become as mysteries, as strange tales, but

rather as the *living Christ,* as the living example for men and women. As a neighbor, as a brother, as a savior, show Him to *this* entity—in that light. 1179-2

The second reading begins:

Cleopas—one who walked on the road to Emmaus.
We are given here the records of that entity . . . known as . . . Susane.
It is well that something be understood of the history or the background of the entity's environs or surroundings.
In the period there had been those appointed from Rome as collectors of the various forms of tax as imposed upon and collected from the people.
Cleopas was among those that were of the faith of the peoples at that time, as had been Matthew.
Hence it was in that environ or that shadow, as may be termed, of one professing a faith in the teachings of the Scribes and Pharisees, yet *collecting* the tribute for a power over the peoples.
This brought condemnation to many of the household, then, from those who adhered more to the orthodox manner of living or activity. Yet the entity, Susane, was one that grew up during that period of the early life of the Master in the earth; acquainted with those of the household of Joseph and Mary. For the entity was of the city of Capernaum at that time.
As to the comparative ages, the entity then was near the age of the sister of the Master; and there were the close acquaintanceships and friendships, though there were the varied degrees of associations, owing to those questions as arose in the various groups that were of the synagogue activities. There were the close companionships, though, until there were the separations owing to the varied manners of the education of the two.
Hence the entity knew a great deal about the happenings in that household. The acquaintanceship with Jude and James was also a part of the entity's experience; though

the entity, more than most of the holy women—as they were eventually called years afterward—followed the teachings of the Master under the varied circumstances; being in the areas about Bethsaida in that period of the expression manifested when there was the feeding of the five thousand, and when there were the rebukings of the peoples that were about Judas at that time.

In the beginning the entity Susane rather favored the manner in which those groups about Judas sought to proclaim Jesus as the deliverer of the peoples from that bondage, that taxation.

This brought to the entity condemnation from her own groups of people. Then with those changes as came about by the shifting of the ministry of the Master to the area closer about Jerusalem, the entity joined with those activities at Bethany.

Thus the entity in the latter portion of His ministry was near to, and present at, those demonstrations of His power over death. And those activities of the entity with Mary, Martha, and the closer associations that later came with the Mother of the Master, after the crucifixion and Resurrection, brought the periods of the greater development.

For, after the Pentecost, when there were the establishings of the ministering to the needs of the peoples far and near, the entity sought, felt, realized the real purposes in those tenets, those expressions of the Master through His periods of ministry in the earth.

Through the days of the teachings of those who followed Stephen, Philip, Barnabas, Paul—all of these were a portion of the entity's relationships.

The activities of the entity were the more constant in the ministry to the physical, the mental and spiritual needs of those throughout her sojourn in the land during those periods following the Crucifixion, those periods of the construction and the applications of the early church.

The entity was not one that would in this day or period be termed a nun, but one ministering firsthand as nurse, as one working with the hands, as one giving counsel, as well as collecting and distributing from the sources of activities through that experience.

When there were the persecutions, and the dispersing of those who had gathered in Jerusalem, the entity was among those in the church in Laodicea, and under the association with Lucius, Mark, Luke, Paul. There the entity remained to be established as one of the first of the deaconesses of that church. There the entity remained throughout the period of its earthly experience, giving a great deal of self in the carrying on of the activities and the establishing of the ministry of the Holy One.

Through the period the entity gained, save in that period when there was the desire for material gains from the persecutions of the political natures. For, as indicated, with the full concept of the purposes, the hopes, the desires, the wishes—as it were—to be expressed by Him—who is the way, the truth, the light—the life was given as a minister to the needs of those who sought to know the truth that maketh men free indeed, though they may be under the shadow of a service to a higher power materially.

Much of those activities in the entity's service were through the ministering to those who were without the faith.   1179-8

One other Susana, not named as a holy woman but still of interest, lived during the time of Jesus. She was the daughter of Vesta (1523) and Lucius (294) at that time.

The entity then was among those of the household of faith, for the entity then was the offspring of one chosen as the minister and teacher in the church at Laodicea. There the entity was the bone of contention between some of those of the church and some of those peoples, in that period of disturbance between Paul, Barnabas, Lucius and his household. For the entity then was of the household of Lucius knowing of and yet not wholly aware of those contentions that arose.

And the questioning of the purpose of men arose from that experience. For the way of a man with a maid, as the preacher gave, is not understood by others; only by the individual, according to the purpose within.

The name then was Susana.   3685-1

Chapter 10

Holy Women Named Salome

*T*hree women named Salome appear as holy women. The first and most prominent of the three is Mary Salome. She is the daughter of Sobe and Solomon, the granddaughter of Ismeria and Eliud, the sister of Eliud, the niece of Anna, and the cousin of Mary. She marries Zebedee and becomes the mother of Roael, James the Greater, Naomi, and John. Roael and Naomi are not mentioned by Emmerich, but both appear in the Cayce readings.

The Cana wedding feast is the first place Jesus performs a miracle at the request of his mother when the wine supplies run short. Emmerich says the groom is Nathanael. Cayce tells at length about a bride named Clana and a groom named Roael. There is no explanation for this difference. This interesting information comes from Cayce reading 5749-15:

> . . . there was the wedding in Cana of Galilee.
> The girl was a relative of those close to the mother of Jesus, who prepared the wedding feast—as was the custom in that period, and is yet among those of the Jewish faith who adhere to the traditions as well as custom of

those people chosen as the channel because of their purpose with God.

The girl [Clana, 609] to be wed was a daughter of the
cousin of Mary, a daughter of a younger sister of Elizabeth,
whose name was also Mary. And she was the one spoken
of as "the other Mary," and not as some have supposed.

The customs required that there be a feast, which was
composed of the roasted lamb with the herbs, the breads
that had been prepared in the special ways as were the
custom and tradition of those who followed close to the
faith in Moses' law, Moses' custom, Moses' ordinances.

The families of Mary were present, as well as those of
the groom.

The groom, in the name Roael, was among the sons of
Zebedee; being an elder brother of James and John who
later became the close friends and the closer followers of
Jesus.   5749-15

Of Clana her reading says:

> The entity then, as Clana, was the bride for whom the first
> of the miracles was performed by Mary's son who became
> the Christ, the Lord.
>
> In that experience we find the entity gained through-
> out, for—as there were the associations with those that
> were of the household of the carpenter and of the fisher-
> men in Cana and in Capernaum, and later in Galilee—the
> entity gained in the understanding and the relationships
> that grew and grew with the women that followed in the
> way.   609-1

As to "The other Mary," another reading gives us this information:

> The entity was among those of the household that enter-
> tained the Master oft; then being an aid to "Mrs. Zebedee,"
> as would be ordinarily termed. John and James were
> charges or cares of the entity during that experience, and

the entity was among those spoken of and referred to as "The other Mary," when no other indication is given as to the place from which the entity came, or as to the groups to which the entity belonged.

These brought the entity close in contact with the holy women. Especially during those periods following the crucifixion, the entity became acquainted the better with the mother. For, as the mother became a part of that care, that charge of John, the associations became close.   2946-2

A later reading for this Mary states:

We find that the entity was among those of the group selected as channels considered worthy for the incoming of the promise of God with man. Know, in thine heart of hearts, as bodies and minds are drawn together, these are not purposeless but purposeful; that the glory of God may be made manifest. For, as has been interpreted correctly, the sons of Zebedee were among those sufficiently able financially, as would be termed in the present, to leave their work, their home (and all of the apostles, save Matthew); for these, the sons of Zebedee, were in favor with those in political authority.

In those periods, then, when there had been the crucifixion, the entity was drawn closer in association physically with the mother of Jesus, the Lord.

When there had been those activities by those pronouncements made upon the cross, they became then as bosom friends.

He, then, is indeed the way, the truth, the light. And, as indicated to the entity in the latter portion (for the entity lived to be of great age, even in that experience—and many may be the years of active service of the entity in its magnifying among men) that which is addressed to her by John in the letter for the "lady elect" [II John 1].

This indicates that reverence which the beloved of the Master held for the entity through that experience.

2946-3

Although there is no indication that Naomi became one of the holy women, her readings give us information and insight into the family of Zebedee and Mary Salome. Her reading says:

> The entity then was among those that came under those influences in the sojourns of the Master in that land of Galilee; for the entity was then a daughter of Zebedee and a sister to those that were close in the activities of the Master in that land.
>
> Through that experience the entity gained in soul development. While fears and doubts arose at times from the activities through the periods of persecution, that sojourn has builded and does make for those abilities to arouse in others those things that may be helpful in their mental and physical self; also that purposefulness in the inmost self that may bring to the entity those satisfying things that bring joy, peace and harmony. And oft in the visions have there come periods when the entity has walked close with those during that sojourn . . .   540-1

Another reading states:

> The entity was the daughter of Zebedee and the other Mary. These individuals were not of the rabble, not of the political, not of great *spiritual* influence or force among the associates of the group. While both were of the Jewish faith, as would be termed today, or the Hebraic faith, they were in that position socially which was above that of the ordinary individuals.
>
> For, as we find, these (Mary and Zebedee) were one of the house of Judah, the other of the house or lineage of Levi. Hence the close associations with those of the priesthood. Yet, by and through the associations of Zebedee, there were the contacts with the Essenes and those groups that held rather to a more universality of application of the tenants and teachings of the peoples during the period.
>
> Hence in such an environment we find that the entity entered, during that period just *after* the birth of the Mas-

ter to Joseph and Mary—of the household of Judah. The entity was between James and John. Hence during that period when the Master, Jesus, was in Egypt; the place being outside of Jerusalem nigh unto Bethany. Hence we see how that the environs for Naomi in the early portion of its experience in that land were under a *varied* effect.

Owing to the circumstances of the group to which Zebedee, the father, belonged, this necessitated the choosing of a following or vocation somewhat in keeping with the forefathers—as the *custom* ran. Yet the very location of the house or the dwelling belied or was at variance to the general customs, owing to the political situations not only as to the Roman rule but because of the edicts that had become rather contrariwise or at variance with—or at cross-purposes with Herod's ruling then of the portions of Judea that later became known as the Galilean or the Samaritan or a questioned peoples.

The activities of Zebedee required that the purposes and aims be rather carried on through or by agents. Or, to put in the parlance of the present, the entity was rather in the fishing business as a wholesaler, than being in active service himself. As indicated or given, that as He passes by He saw James and John with their father Zebedee mending their nets, rather were the brothers of Naomi and the father *supervising* and reasoning with the employees as to their activities. For, remember the situations:

Mary, the mother, was of the priesthood that was renounced by the cousin, John the Baptist, as known; yet the activities with the Essenes demanded (as would be termed in the present) the keeping secret the meetings of the peoples or adherents during those cross-purposed edicts of the Roman ruler and Herod. But after the death of Herod the Great, when Herod the Less became in power in the political forces, more consideration was brought or given to those who called their meetings in those various manners. These activities came about, then, when Naomi was nigh unto thirty years of age. . .

As to the surroundings, we find that the entity's home

life was out of the ordinary—even in that period of experience. For it was pulled, as it were, *between* the teachings
or the training of the mother and the activities of the father and the brother; yet it had associations in the Roman
activities, as *well* as a position in the Jewish faith or Jewish
activity.

Hence we find this as a description of the body:

One educated in the schools of those that were the
teachers from Carmel, yet associated with those activities
of the people about the temple—and those who dedicated
themselves to the service that was to bring those activities
which to the world today find themselves exemplified in
many ways; in one the sisters of the orders known as the
Catholic—or the Church—in the present; in the other the
orthodox activities of the sisters of mercy among certain
Jewish sects.

These, then, may give the *conditions*—of the activity in
which the entity, Naomi, in its teen years, found itself;
pulled between whether the holy activities of the Essenes
or the dedicating of self to the faith of the fathers.

When there first began those activities among John's
teachings, we find the entity then joined rather with those
of the Essene group. For John first taught that the women
who *chose* might dedicate their lives to a specific service.

Hence not only the brothers but those employed by the
brothers (Peter, Andrew and Judas—not Iscariot) joined in
the activities. These were of the fisherfolk who aided in
establishing the teachings in and among the people, that
held to *both* the old and the new environs.   540-4

These readings help to give a better idea of the financial, social, and
spiritual opportunities of the Zebedee family.

As we turn again to Mary Salome, she seems to be close to her Aunt
Anna, who sends for her and two other women when she is about to
give birth to Mary. The other two are Anna's sister, Maraha, and Enue,
Elizabeth's sister (ACE 1 149). At that time Mary Salome does not yet
have her sons James and John. Mary Heli, Anna's first born is not present

for Mary's birth, but Mary Cleophas (Mary Heli's daughter and Anna's little granddaughter) is present soon after the birth touching the new baby. What a very special honor for Mary Salome to be invited to the birth of Mary.

The next reference to Mary Salome is as one of the holy women staying at an inn between the desert Gibea and the desert Ephraim, about five hours from Bethany, along with the Blessed Virgin, Mary Cleophas, the Widow Lea, and Johanna Chusa. They stay in an enclosed shed with two apartments divided off into alcoves with some male attendants sleeping by a fire in an open hut in front of the shed. Jesus is at Lazarus', and the women go there the next day and spend time with Martha (ACE 1 401).

Perhaps Mary Salome is most famous for a request she makes of Jesus. Jesus is very busy with a huge crowd of people near Bethabara on the Jordan. He blesses many children, heals many sick, and goes on to visit a house full of lepers. The Apostles who are with Him dread contact with the lepers and go on ahead to wait under a tree. In this manner, Jesus continues on His way, healing as He goes and instructing groups. The disciples are with Him, helping and observing and making suggestions. When two brothers want Jesus to settle an argument over a patrimony, He tells them it is not His business. John and Peter think He should solve the problem, and Jesus tells them He came to distribute heavenly goods not earthly ones. Then he launches into a long exhortation to the gathering crowd. The Apostles have not received the Holy Ghost and so are focused on an earthly kingdom. There is some discussion about this subject among the Apostles. They simply do not understand much that Jesus tells the crowd about His Kingdom soon to come. Also, during this time period, messengers arrive to urge Jesus to go to the very ill Lazarus. Before He reaches Bethany, Mary Salome, with her sons beside her, approaches Jesus. Noting that He has just announced that His mission will soon be fulfilled, Mary requests that He do the proper thing—appoint His own relatives to the most important posts. She asks that John and James be placed at His right and left hands. Jesus quite sternly rebukes her and tells her she has no idea what she is requesting for her sons (ACE 3 471, 482)

Mary Salome is in Jerusalem at the time of the Paschal feast and walking and talking with Magdalen, Martha, Mary Cleophas, Salome, and the Mother of Jesus. They seem to be uneasy—as though they expect something to happen. They have stopped in at the house of Mary Marcus but soon go out to seek more news. Then Lazarus, Nicodemus, and Joseph of Arimathea cross their path and try to reassure them, but Mary tells them of Judas's restlessness and sudden departure and feels he does not have good intentions. They go back to the house of Mary Marcus (ACE 4 88).

The arrest of Jesus occurs, and He is being painfully dragged to court. The disciples disperse when about fifty soldiers come to escort the procession and prevent a riot. The group of women who include Mary Cleophas, Martha, Magdalen, Susanna, Veronica, Salome, Johanna Chusa, Mary Marcus, the Blessed Virgin, and Mary Salome head toward the Valley of Josaphat, south of Gethsemane. Lazarus, John Mark, and sons of Veronica and Simeon are with them (ACE 4 126). During these sorrowful proceedings, people carry on conversations in the streets and make malicious remarks about various followers of Jesus. They say how women such as Johanna Chusa, Susanna, John Mark's mother Mary, and Salome surely do regret having anything to do with Jesus and will certainly be humbled (ACE 4 135).

At the foot of the cross, Mary the Mother of Jesus hears Him pray, "Father, forgive them, for they know not what they do!" She presses forward to hear her Son, and John, Salome, and Mary Cleophas came right behind her to protect her, but the captain of the guard does not stop her (ACE 4 285).

Then as the four men carry the body of Jesus on the litter, Emmerich names three different Salome's as following along to the tomb. The list includes the Blessed Virgin, Mary Heli, Magdalen, Mary Cleophas, Veronica, Johanna Chusa, Mary Marcus, the wife of Zebedee (Mary Salome), Salome of Jerusalem, Anna (a niece of St. Joseph), Susanna, and Salome (ACE 4 339). There is another specific mention of Salome going to the city with some of the other holy women to buy embalming items (ACE 4 360). The next morning very early Magdalen, Mary Cleophas, Johanna Chusa, and Salome carry the various spices, herbs, oils, etc. for

Jesus' body to the gate of Nicodemus on their way to the tomb (ACE 4 365). The nun explains that Salome and Magdalen share the expense of the items purchased for Jesus' burial. She makes this point clear by saying that the Salome of whom she speaks is not the mother of James and John but rather a wealthy widow and resident of Jerusalem, a niece of St. Joseph (ACE 4 367). Therefore, it is no doubt the same Salome who follows Magdalen at a distance into the area of the tomb and then goes rushing to tell the other women of the empty tomb while Magdalen hurries to the disciples.

This suggests that Salome of Jerusalem is a relative of Joseph. Additional references to Salome support this conclusion. When Jesus is going with Lazarus to Bethany, three holy women walk out an hour's distance to meet them. A widow named Salome is with Magdalen and Martha and lives with Martha. The nun provides additional information that, like Susanna, Salome is related to the holy family through one of Joseph's five brothers and that she is present at the interment of Jesus (ACE 3 188). She also is the Salome present with the holy women at Mary Marcus' house when they (including Mary Salome) go out to learn of what is happening with Jesus (ACE 4 88).

There is still another Salome among the holy women. She may be the one in an Edgar Cayce reading:

> There we find the entity came under those influences and activities of the Master Himself, as well as being among those who aided in the establishing of those who went about ministering—through the activities in those periods following the Crucifixion, the Resurrection, and the days of Pentecost.
>
> For the entity was among those spoken of as the Holy Women, that attended those activities following the experiences; first the entity coming in contact with those activities and the death *and* the raising of Lazarus, and later with Elizabeth, Mary, Salome, Mary of Magda, Martha—all of those were a part of the experiences of the entity—as Salome . . .
>
> There we find the entity gaining the greater through the

> services and activities as a seamstress, or a maker of linen or tatting, or laces, during those experiences.
>
> And through those activities the entity brought into the experiences of others assurances of help through confidences, through the activities that brought hope to those who were discouraged.   1874-1

Yet another Salome may be the daughter of Jairus. The girl's name is Salome, and the nun's visions certainly expand on the well-known biblical story.

Jesus is teaching and healing and the disciples go in the evening to their families. Jesus goes near Capernaum to His mother's house. All the holy women are there, and all are joyful. Mary tells Jesus that the Centurion Cornelius is a good man with a sick slave. She also petitions Jesus to cure Salome, daughter of the Elder of the synagogue. Jesus cures the slave by a word because Cornelius has such faith. Jairus appears in the square before the synagogue and implores Jesus to come to his rapidly failing daughter. Before Jesus can go to the house near where Cornelius lives, a messenger arrives with the news that Salome has died. Jesus reassures Jairus that He can still heal the girl. Already mourners are gathering before the house. Jesus takes Peter, James the Greater, and John toward the girl's room. He tells people not to lament as she is only sleeping. They laugh at Him, but He orders the court cleared and locked. He proceeds with the three Apostles and the parents. The nun feels the mother lacks confidence so that she acts coldly. The father is not really a friend of Jesus either because he is very much a Pharisee. He reasons that if Jesus succeeds, he has his daughter. If Jesus fails, it will be a triumph for the Pharisees. Still he is impressed that Jesus cured Cornelius's servant.

The girl is small for eleven. Jesus raises the girl in His arms, holds her on His chest and breathes on her. The nun is amazed to see a ball of light with a figure inside on the right side of the corpse. As Jesus breathes on Salome, the figure takes a human form of light and enters her mouth. Then Jesus places the girl on her couch, takes her by the wrist and says, "Damsel, arise!" She sits up. Jesus leads her to her parents. They have been quite skeptical; now they are quite ecstatic. Jesus tells them to feed the child and not to make a big outcry over the situation. The father thanks Jesus, but the mother barely says thanks. Jesus discusses the case with the three Apostles as they leave. He tells them the girl arises for her own sake and for the glory of the Kingdom of God. She is guiltless but must now save her soul from death. The Pharisees immediately accuse Jesus of sorcery. Jesus prays long that night (ACE 3 1, 36).

Cornelius tells Jesus He is giving a feast for his cured servant and will make many burnt offerings of animals. Jesus tells him instead to invite his enemies and make them friends and lead them to the truth. Invite the poor and feed the food to them instead of making burnt offerings. Cornelius does as Jesus says.

Time passes. Jesus preaches and cures. At Peter's house He teaches a large crowd and heals a paralytic man by telling him his sins are forgiven. This infuriates the Pharisees, who say only God can forgive sins. Jairus observes this healing. Salome is again fatally ill, and according to the nun, the illness is a punishment for the sins of the parents and daughter. They treat her healing in a frivolous manner, have no gratitude, and make no changes in lifestyle. Jairus does not object to the ways of his beautiful, vain wife. Jesus is a laughing matter to them, and Salome follows their bad examples. A terrible fever attacks her and leaves her delirious. The parents suspect they are to blame. At last, they turn to Jesus asking for pity. Jairus falls on his knees and pleads for Jesus to come. A messenger comes saying the girl is dead. It is at this point that the woman with the blood issue touches Jesus' robe and is instantly cured. Jesus is aware and asks who is touching Him. The woman admits she knows He can cure her if she can just touch His garment. Jairus observes this with awe and then takes Jesus to his house.

This time Jesus does not say Salome is only sleeping. He takes the parents, the grandmother, and Peter, James, and John into the room with the corpse. Jesus asks for a branch and a container of water, which he blesses. Then He dips the branch into the water and sprinkles the corpse. Next, He takes the girl by the hand and tells her to arise. Again, the nun sees the dark globe containing the girl's soul enter her mouth. Jesus leads her to her parents and gives them a very strong sermon on their faulty lives. He advises them on how to change, and warns them that if they do not do so, they may cause the death of the soul. The girl cries. Jesus advises her not to sin with her eyes or in any other way. While she has some grapes and bread, He tells her to do penance, pray, do good works, and reject worldliness. He also says to be still about the miracle and reflect on God's mercy. He does this for the Apostles as well so that they will do their healing through love—love for God and not their own glory (ACE 3 65-70).

Jairus changes his ways completely, divides his wealth, giving one third to the poor and one third to the Community, and keeps the last third for the family (ACE 3 74, 94, 208).

Salome becomes very pious and marries Saraseth, a scribe from Nazareth and a disciple of Jesus. Both join the Community. Therefore, I believe it is quite possible that Jairus' daughter is another Salome among the holy women.

However, there exists another possibility concerning the fourth Salome—one that involves a Jairus who is a captain of a guard whose daughter, Touhpar, is also raised from death. Because Maipah, her mother, is designated as a holy woman, their story deserves to be told. The following readings address this:

> The entity [Maipah] was in the Palestine land, during those periods when the Master walked in the earth; and the entity was aware of those influences of His life in that experience.
>
> For was not the entity then the mother of Jairus' daughter [559?] who became aware of His presence to heal body, mind and soul? . . .
>
> How much more, then, may thy body in the present find in thy arms that which may indeed be the channel to tell the story of His love for man, of His filling the whole life purpose of man! How well does such fit the entity to tell to those who are young and old, the stories of the patience of the man of Galilee—yea, of how stern He might be when He put the entity out of the room, as well as those of the household, because of doubt—and as to putting the whole trust in the faith of Him that *is* the way and light and truth and understanding!

The entity was a joy to many throughout that experience; suffering oft in disputations—being disturbed oft by the other individuals who caused the disturbance—and yet the entity in heart and mind was at peace because of His blessings to thee!

Hold fast to that as ye gained in seeing in body the love in the flesh presented to thy arms, by the love of the Son of the Father, God!   1968-1

More information appears in a later reading:

The entity was among the daughters of the children of Ishmael. And the associations, the wedding with Jairus in the early portion of the entity's experience in the earth plane, came through the journeying of Jairus with those influences established in the western portion of the country now known as Turkey; and the activities of the entity through those experiences were of a social as well as political nature.

There was quite a variation as to the position of women in a household as was the entity, Maipah, and those in a household of those in authority—as was Jairus, because of his position politically. He was not merely the captain of a guard, or of a garrison, but as one who was in authority pertaining to the supplying of the commercial, the social, and the political relationships of the land; when the entity joined in the activities, in portions of that now known as the Galilean land . . .

The entity was some twenty years of age when the first child was born; then the second and third—and the third child was the daughter, Touhpar by name.

When the companion or husband, Jairus, became aware of the teachings and tenets of the Master, Jesus of Nazareth, and knowing the conditions surrounding the companion and the "delicate" condition (as would be called), for there was the expectancy of the fourth child to be born—the anxiety as manifested brought the commendation from the Master, as well as wonderment from his associates or companions in his office. This showed rather the unusual interest of man for his mate, and for the offspring, for the period or time. But Jairus had been influenced by those tenets which he had heard expressed, not only by John but by the followers of—and the Master Himself.

This brought into the experience of the entity, Maipah, that of humbleness, patience, desire for expression in some manner. Yet, because of the early teaching, the early training, wonderment and fear and doubt were also a part of the consciousness through that particular period.

And it was that period, and that following—as to what the entity did about it—which brings the urges within the manifested activities of the entity in the present.

For, with the coming of the Master to the home, and with the conditions and environs of self as well as the counsel of advice of others, there came doubt and fear. Yet with the command that those who would hinder by their adverse thought or expressions be put away, the entity and companion had their loved one given again to them as a *living* example of His indeed being the resurrection.

Thus the entity sought to know and aid those who were the leaders or teachers—of course, the holy women, the prophetesses, and those who had been instrumental in every form or manner in keeping the tenets alive in the experience of others.

Throughout the rest of its sojourn, then, the entity lent self in aid of every manner; in the social manner as well as in the *practical* helpfulness to all who sought to keep the faith.

The entity lived to a ripe age for those periods, and the persecutions. But being of those in authority the entity was protected or shielded in some ways; for, with others that came to know more of the blessings to be had materially and mentally from the embracing of those principles and tenets of the teacher, greater opportunities came for the entity throughout its sojourn.

For, who sought physical associations with those who

were of the low caste, or low estate, save as applied to the mothers of faith, those of the holy women, through that experience, of which the entity was one!   1968-4

Next, is the Cayce reading for Jairus' daughter:

The entity then was that one whom the Master called again from the deep sleep—Jairus' daughter. Before and after that happening, we find that the entity was one in the experience who gave much of self to make for the closer association and relation with the mental attributes of the spirit as related to the material things, rather than to the thoughts of material things themselves.   559-7

In another relevant reading Cayce states:

The entity then in that period when the Master passed through the land, and the entity [was of] the one[s] to whom the Master spoke and said, "Arise, maiden," [to] then the daughter of Jairus. In this experience the entity gained, and in the present ever the desire to know more of that love, that force, as emanated through that experience, has the entity sought much—and those influences as have to do with powers of the innate influence does the entity seek, yet fears from within. Here would the entity dwell long upon that experience, could the entity draw much from that experience, and ever does there appear to the entity a peculiar sensation when that is read.   2485-1

This point Cayce clarifies in another reading:

(Q) Please clarify information in my life reading regarding the experience as wife of Jairus. Was I the mother of the entity now known as [421], or the entity now known as [2485]?
(A) The entity was one of the wives of Jairus, see, and the mother of that entity now called [42l]. The entity [2485]

was then also a wife of Jairus, but not the mother of the
daughter that was healed; rather being desirous that *her*
daughter receive a blessing and because of seeming indif-
ference or change, brought disturbance to *both* entities
for a period.   1968-8

This reading given for Jairus' daughter continues:

During that period when the Master walked in the land.
The entity then of the household of the ruler to *whom* the
entity [the Master] came, and the entity heard that Voice
that *called* the entity [559] back to service in that experience, "Talitha, Talitha, Arise!" the daughter of Jairus in that
experience. *Gaining* throughout, for the service as ren-
dered to others through that life, that hope, that understanding, given by that touch . . .   421-5

Thus, the various entities named Salome receive recognition as holy
women.

Chapter 11

The Three Widows of Nazareth and the Widow f Nain

The three widows of Nazareth are Seba, Lea, and Mara. Seba and Lea are daughters of Sobe, Anna's sister. Mara is a daughter of Rhoda (ACE 1 493), who is a sister of Elizabeth. Rhoda has three daughters and two sons. One daughter is one of the three widows (Mara, Mary?), and the two sons become Jesus' disciples. One of Rhoda's sons marries Maroni, but they have no children. Then the widowed Maroni marries a nephew of Anna named Eliud (son of Sobe), and their son is Martial. When Eliud dies, Maroni becomes known as the Widow of Nain (ACE 2 455). Mary is apparently one of Rhoda's daughters as she is called a niece of Elizabeth. She becomes a widow, goes to Nazareth, and then goes to Capernaum. She is present at the death of the Virgin Mary (ACE 1 357).

There is really not much information about the three widows. Sometimes they are named individually, sometimes as a group, and sometimes simply referred to as one of the widows. Also, they are, according to the nun, mistaken for one another frequently.

Once Jesus is visiting with Eliud, the elderly Essenian, who with his family, takes care of Mary's house near Nazareth when she is away.

Meanwhile some holy women gather with Mary in her home. They are Mary Cleophas, her niece; Johanna Chusa, a cousin of Anna the Prophetess; the widow Lea; and Mary Marcus (ACE 1 366).

Another time, Lea is specified as arriving with the Blessed Virgin at Martha's house in Bethany along with six other holy women (Ace 1 405).

When Jesus is talking to people in Peter's home, Lea is there. Her sister-in-law, Enue, is cured of an issue of blood by Jesus just prior to this gathering. Lea is greatly impressed with Jesus' teaching. She moves about the crowd so that she can proclaim her reverence for Jesus. Mother Mary and several holy women enter. Lea sees Mary and cries out as to how blessed she is to be Jesus' mother. Jesus quietly comments that those who hear God's word and keep it are more blessed. Lea goes to Mary, tells her of Enue's cure, and tells Mary she, Lea, wants to give her wealth to the Community (ACE 3 73, 74).

Lea appears on another occasion in Capernaum when Jesus is teaching. She wears a veil and keeps repeating the statement about the blessed womb that bore Jesus and Jesus' response of how more blessed are those who hear God's word and keep it. She has come to visit the holy women and bring rich gifts to the Community (ACE 3 307, 308).

Once, Mary the Mother is traveling with a group from a shepherd village near Sichem to Bethany. One servant precedes the women while the other follows. They walk single file because of narrow paths and obstacles such as stones, brush, etc., which the servants move aside and then replace after all pass. The four holy women with Mary are Mary Salome, Johanna Chusa, Mary Cleophas, and one of the three widows. This is a rather typical way of referring to the widows rather than naming each individually (ACE 1 394).

Seba, daughter of Sobe is given as the mother of Kolaiah, a disciple of Jesus (ACE 1 360), and of Nathanael, the bridegroom of Cana (ACE 2 34). Other times she is simply referred to as the bridegroom's mother. Apparently Lea is the widow referred to in another place as the maternal aunt of the bridegroom (ACE 2 44).

The widows are again named when the Blessed Virgin, Mary Cleophas, the wife of James the Greater, and two of the widows anticipate Jesus' arrival at the shepherd huts where they wait all day for Him (ACE 2 190).

Since the widows' sons appear listed in the index of the Emmerich books simply as sons of the widows, there is confusion about to whom Sirach and Eustachius belong (ACE 1 349 and ACE 2 260, 485). The sons of the widows are listed in the Volume 2 index as Eustachius, Kolaja, and Sirach. Colaya is Lea's son (ACE 2 372). Note that there is a difference in spelling which also contributes to the confusion. The persons Kolaiah/Kolaia and Colaya/Kolaia are the same person. Colaya's mother asks Jesus to admit the other sons as disciples. After the death of Jesus, these sons are ordained to the priesthood by Bishop Joses Barsabas at Eleutheropolis.

The widow of Nain, Maroni, is the sister of James the Greater's wife. Andrew and Nathanael tell her that Jesus is coming to Nain. He arrives at an inn outside the city and with another widow Maroni goes to meet Jesus. The veiled women kneel at Jesus' feet. The widow of Nain urges Jesus to accept the other widow's gift of all she possesses for the treasury of the holy women to care for the disciples and the poor, whom she desires to serve. Jesus accepts the offer. They have a meal from the provisions the women bring, and the disciples receive the money to take to the women's treasury at Capernaum (ACE 2 205).

Next Jesus goes to Nain—about seven hours distant. The woman giving her possessions tells Jesus of a widow named Mary, who wants to give over her possessions, too. Jesus asks that the gift be given later as needed. The woman's case is involved and includes adultery, a devil possession, and supplication to Mary for help from Jesus (ACE 2 206).

Rhoda, mother of Mara, one of the three widows, has a son who marries Maroni. They have no children, and he dies. Then Maroni, following the Jewish law, marries a nephew of Anna named Eliud, son of Sobe. They have a son named Martial. Eliud dies, and Maroni becomes known as the widow of Nain (Ace 2 455).

In the valley of Capernaum, Saturnin baptizes and names Maroni's son Martial. The holy women stay with Maroni and do not go to the instruction Jesus gives. Instead, they join in the baptismal feast of her son (ACE 3 61).

Jesus and several disciples go to an inn near Damna. Maroni is there with the pagan, Lais of Nain. Previously, at Meroz, Jesus frees her two daughters from devil possession, caused by the sins of the parents. Maroni's son Martial is very ill, and she begs Jesus to come and heal her twelve–year–old son as she fears he will die before she can get back to him. Jesus tells her to go home in peace; He will come but does not say when. Maroni has to travel about nine hours and leaves at once leaving behind many gifts for the inn. She is a very wealthy woman and most generous, especially with the poor children in Nain, where she is greatly loved. She has great faith in Jesus because she is a witness to His curing many. She is also present when Jesus heals Mary Cleophas (ACE 2 3, 5).

According to Luke 7:11–16, Jesus teaches as he travels to Nain with about thirty disciples. It is a delightful place with nice houses and beautiful scenes on all sides and the area is rich in fruit, wine, and grain. Maroni owns a mountain filled with vineyards.

It is morning when Jesus and disciples reach Nain and see the funeral procession coming toward them. The coffin rests on a frame attached to poles with four men carrying it. The coffin is in the shape of a body and looks like a covered, woven basket. Jesus passes through the disciples, lined up on either side of the road and commands the funeral procession to stop and set the coffin down. They do so. The veiled women are following the coffin with Maroni in front, weeping. Jesus tells her very kindly not to weep. Then he asks for a small branch and water. Water and a twig of hyssop quickly appear. Jesus has the bearers open the coffin and remove all but one linen covering from the body. Then Jesus looks to heaven and talks earnestly to His Father. Jesus blesses the water, dips the branch into it and sprinkles the crowd. The nun sees numerous small figures like black birds, snakes, beetles, and toads coming from the onlookers. She sees the crowd become purer and lighter. Next Jesus sprinkles the corpse and makes the sign of the cross over the boy. At that motion, a black, cloudy form escapes the body, and Jesus says to Martial, "Arise." The boy sits up and looks around in amazement. Jesus requests clothing, and someone places a mantle around Martial, who then gets to his feet asking what he is doing there. Jesus leads him to his mother. As Maroni hugs him joyfully, Jesus tells her that she has her son back. But Jesus warns that once the boy receives baptism and regeneration, He shall reclaim him.

All follow to Maroni's home singing a hymn of praise. Jesus and the disciples follow and enter her large house surrounded by gardens and courts. The attendants bathe Martial and dress him in a white tunic. They wash the feet of Jesus and the disciples and serve them refreshments. Then a huge distribution of gifts to the poor takes place. Jesus instructs the crowd in the court yard. Martial runs about joyously with some children approaching him cautiously and others acting as though they are seeing a ghost. Peter, the widow's relative (she is the daughter of the brother of Peter's father-in-law) is quite happy and at home in this house and rather serves as father of the family.

Jesus presents some quite interesting comments on death, the importance of virtuous parents, and Israel's present position. He says that Israel is like one standing on the edge of a grave due to sin and mental blindness. He continues with His analogies of the Jews rejecting the Son of God as analogous to being the opposite of the opening of the coffin and freeing Martial from death. The crowd has a variety of reactions to what they witness. The nun notes that as Jesus sprinkles the blessed water on Martial, she sees shadows of loathsome vermin rise from the body and go into the earth. In contrast, other raisings of the dead involve calling back the soul in the vessel associated with the deeds of the entity. At Jesus' call the soul hovers and then reenters the body so that the dead awake. However, in Martial's case, it is as though death—a dead weight, is lifted from the body.

Many people come to Nain for healings, and the next morning Jesus cures many, including numerous broken marriages. He demonstrates the indissolubility of marriage by pouring together milk and water and tells those asking Him to allow divorce that He will do so if they can separate the milk from the water. He tells them Moses allowed divorces because of the obduracy of the Jews. But one flesh cannot be divided, and even if the couple does not live together, the husband must support the children and wife. The couple may not marry any others. Jesus goes then to the homes of those requesting divorces and does some very grand counseling—so grand that the couples become reunited and

live happily together. The Pharisees, in their attempt to entrap Jesus
with a charge of teaching a false doctrine cannot fault Him and are
furious in their failure and His success (ACE 3 11–18).

Later, the Widow of Nain assists the Blessed Virgin, Lazarus, Martha,
Dina, and Mary the Suphanite in a huge distribution of provisions,
material, and ready–made clothes. This takes place at an instruction
Jesus gives on the mountain of Gabara where the people gather in
camps with those from the same district, putting up tents together (ACE
3 319).

The Pharisees (over sixty in number) come from various districts to
gather in Capernaum. On the way, they inquire about Jesus' most amazing cures and order people, especially those healed and their witnesses
to appear in Capernaum for questioning. Among others, they order the
presence of Cornelius and his servant, Jairus and family, the widow of
Nain and Martial, and numerous witnesses. When their plans and in-
terrogations do not disprove Jesus' miracles, they fall back on accusing
Him of dealing with the devil. They charge Him with being involved
with dissolute women, rousing people almost to the point of treason,
profaning the Sabbath, and causing alms to cease flowing to the synagogues (ACE 3 206).

Again, Jesus and some disciples go to Nain. Several disciples and
Martial, the resurrected youth, come to meet Jesus and His followers
near the well outside the city. These disciples and some of the holy
women come from Jerusalem and others come from Nazareth with Mary
after celebrating the feast of Pentecost. Jesus goes to an inn situated in a
house belonging to the widow of Nain, Maroni. He goes to see her. She
comes out veiled to meet Him and kneels at His feet. Five women are
present with Maroni: Martha, Magdalen, Mary the Suphanite, Veronica,
and Johanna Chusa. Jesus tells the holy women about the Cyprus experience and about the reception by which the Roman Governor in
Salamis honors Him. The Pharisees in Nain do nothing special for Jesus.
They do not like the way He attracts the poor, miserable people they
normally discard.

Jesus spends time with His disciples and tells them very clearly of the
sufferings and persecutions ahead. They weep at the prospect. Then,

they go into Maroni's garden to join the holy women. Jesus tells them of the reconciliations among the troubled married couples in Mallep. When He and the disciples leave the garden to go to the synagogue for the close of the Sabbath, He finds many sick persons waiting for Him on litters. Even at the synagogue they seek cures from Him, and He obliges. As usual, the Pharisees are upset that He heals people on the Sabbath (ACE 3 435–440).

On the way to Bethsaida, Jesus and His disciples come to an inn where His mother, the widow of Nain, and some other women await Him. They want to take leave of Him before He goes to the other side of the Jordan to teach (ACE 3 461).

The Edgar Cayce readings mention the widow of Nain in three readings. One reading tells a woman named Deul when Jesus walked the earth that she ". . . was among those peoples that were aided by the ministry of this teacher, this Master during that sojourn, of those people to whom the entity received back alive the son—as they walked from Nain at those periods of His ministry there." (601-2) An unnamed holy woman at the time of Jesus receives this message: ". . . the entity was in what is now known as the Holy Land and among those who were the courtiers when the widow of Nain was stopped by the Master, among the holy women who were mourners for this particular occasion was the activity of the entity in that particular period, but the application of many of those things which were heard and applied was and is part of the consciousness of the entity, and in these directions only need the application of self to become that which would be a helpful experience for many." (5248-1) And in the third reading, Cayce says that Pegler ". . . was among those who came under the direction of the teachings not only of the Master Himself, but of the apostles; having that deep sympathy with—and in association with—the disciples, the apostles, and the gatherings with those activities during the experience.

"Coming into the experience as a professional mourner, the entity came in contact with the widow of Nain, when the son was delivered again to the mother." (2454-3)

Chapter 12

The Holy Women Related to Peter

The women in Peter's family do not receive very much attention. The Bible tells us about his mother-in-law being healed by Jesus. The nun and prophet tell much more about these women.

One of the twelve maidens dedicated to preparing a channel for Jesus' birth is Andra. She ". . . in the latter portion of the experience in that land, joined in that band who made for what would be termed in the present a prayer band, or ladies' aid or circle, that made preparations for those that had separated themselves to become the followers of those peoples. And the entity then was with Simon Peter's mother, wife, the children of Zebedee, and their families—as well as Thomas and Luke; for Luke and Thomas were brothers." (649-1)

Early in His ministry Jesus keeps the Sabbath near Nazareth and Sephoris in a school between the two places and near a former residence of Anna. Holy women from Nazareth are present, including wives of some future Apostles. Peter's wife is specifically named (ACE 1 350). A short time later, Jesus travels to an area where rich publicans live. They receive Jesus and His followers pleasantly. Several women arrive, and the nun believes Peter's wife is with them. They talk with Jesus and soon leave as they are probably on some mission elsewhere (ACE 1 358).

When Jesus leaves Socoth, He heads toward an inn near Great Chorazin where He is to meet His mother and the holy women. Among the holy women are Peter's wife and Susanna of Jerusalem (ACE 1 481). Jesus travels more and teaches in Ulama where numerous possessed people live. He cures many there. Then the disciples leave the city first so that Jesus can follow unnoticed. They travel all night to reach His mother's house in Capernaum the next morning. Several women are there, including the bride of Cana and Peter's wife and her sister. Mary has a roomy house, and someone is usually with her. Some widows live nearby and holy women and disciples stop by. Jesus teaches at the Capernaum synagogue, and the disciples and holy women attend (ACE 2 93).

Salamar is ". . . among the sisters of Peter's wife, yea, one who received from the Master the care of her sister when Peter's wife's mother was healed." (3357-1) There is also Polias. "The entity then among those of the womenfolk who followed those that were imprisoned during those periods, who were forced to give account of the activities before those in power, and the entity suffered in body and in mind, gained after there had been that suffering and that understanding coming in that there *be* the needs oft that those of the physical must be crucified that the *spiritual* life may be made alive. In the name then Polias, and a follower of him who taught in the catacombs of the city, he who was crucified with his head downward, and a member of his household, being then a *sister* of Peter's wife." (1742-2)

Cleo is a relative of Peter. In a reading, Cayce says that:

> The entity was among those who were later called the holy women—being among the daughters of those who were the leaders, the followers of the Master, Jesus the Christ.
>
> We find that the entity was a niece of Peter—a daughter of Andrew, one of the disciples; and was among those who were active following the crucifixion in caring for the upper chamber where the disciples and those first followers gathered.

The entity then took care of that chamber, as it was there the wife of a brother of John and James, Zebedee's children, and the entity's activities brought blessings to the many, making that chamber as a home, a church, a meeting place, a hopeful experience for those throughout that period—even when the persecutions arose. For the entity then, as Cleo made for those activities that brought hope to the persecuted. Disturbances that arose were counted rather by the entity as blessings, in that they enabled the entity to suffer for its faith.   2154-1

Here is a member of the household of Cleo:

The entity then was among the children of the household of Cleo, the wife of Peter and his peoples; or the one that was set *secondly* as the child blessed by the Master when He said, "Suffer little children to come unto me, and forbid them not, for of such is the kingdom of heaven."

When a soul, then, has been blessed by Him, who *is* Life, how may it ever *wholly* wander from that blessing as given by Life itself? How, when He—*Life*—the *Christ*—has promised in thine own experience that ye are to fill a purpose in the experience of others? If ye will wholly trust in Him, He—and ye—will not fail.

The entity, then, in the name Junie—gained; though in the latter portion came suffering, yet the entity—when Peter came from prison—was among these that, with Rhoda, opened the door to let him in, though the prison door had opened to his touch.

In the experience the entity found that awakening that may be aroused in the present to the associations of that which is the ideal in every soul's experience to be in the earth as a channel of blessings through Him that has blessed thee, that does bless thee, in the activities in a material world. Thus may the greater activity for the entity be aroused in the present.   608-7

Another niece of Peter's appears in the Cayce readings:

> The entity was among those who were present and saw
> Peter's mother-in-law healed. This to the entity, then, has
> never been as a mystery—instantaneous healing. While
> never fully understood, there is the belief and the willing-
> ness to act in that direction without questioning; which is
> latent and manifested as a part of the entity—to be sin-
> cere, to be in the house of faith.
>   In the experience the entity knew many material hard-
> ships, and many of those activities to which those of the
> faith were called through persecution by those in the po-
> litical as well social activities. . . The name then was Ruth;
> and *well* is the name for the entity in the present. The en-
> tity was a niece then of Peter, but *not* Andrew's daugh-
> ter—rather the daughter—of Barjon.   910-4

Another relative connection between the holy women and Peter is
Jonas, the third husband of Mary Cleophas and father of her son Simeon.
Jonas is the young brother of Peter's father-in-law and associated with
him in the fishing business (ACE 3 55).

Peter has a house outside the city and another on a lake. His wife
directs the domestic affairs of the first place, and his mother-in-law and
step-daughter oversee the house on the lake. Jesus meets crowds for
instruction and healing at both places—and also at Peter's fishery (ACE
3 57).

Jesus comes with Peter to his house. The holy women and Blessed
Virgin are present. The disciples wait in the garden or walk on to Mary's
house. Peter's neatly built house has a court in front and a garden. It is
a long house with a walkway on the roof that gives a lovely view of the
lake. The nun comments that she does not see Peter's step-daughter nor
his wife's sons but speculates that they are probably at school. Peter has
no children by his wife. She is, at the moment, with the group of holy
women. Since the stream of Capernaum flows by Peter's house, he can
get in his little one-seated sail boat with his fishing tackle and sail down
to the lake.

Jesus confers with the holy women about the house on the lake they have hired for His and His disciples' use. He encourages them to avoid extravagances as He needs little. He advises them to provide for the house with disciples and poor in mind. Then, He and His disciples leave Peter's house and go to His mother's. After conversing for awhile, He goes away alone to pray (ACE 2 222).

Peter's mother-in-law is tall and thin. She is so sickly that she moves about in the house by leaning on the walls (ACE 2 222). She is told by Cayce:

> The entity was among those of the group called the holy women, or those that saw, that knew many of the associations with the disciples, the apostles, and the helpful, direct influence of the Master himself.
>
> Those periods brought to the entity the closer associations through the latter periods of the activity. For, being healed as it were, physically, by the Master himself, the entity's sojourn in the earth was long and varied, and would make a book in itself.
>
> During that experience the entity had two activities; the growing of plants, especially adaptable for the healing of the body, and flowers; and also the ministering to the sick. Not as a nurse—rather as a comforter. For the entity at periods acted in the capacity as a hired mourner, as was the custom of that period. The name then was Esdrela.
>
> **1541-11**

The disciples urge Jesus to leave Capernaum and go immediately to Peter's in Bethsaida because his mother-in-law has a high fever and is in danger of dying. When Jesus arrives, He goes straight to her room with family members following Him. The nun believes Peter's daughter is among them. Whether she means step-daughter is unclear. Jesus leans on the bed, speaks to Esdrela, and then lays His hands upon her breast and head. She does not move. Jesus stands up, takes her hand and raises her to a sitting position. Then, He requests she be given something to drink. The daughter brings a little cup in the form of a boat.

Jesus blesses the drink, and Esdrela drinks. Jesus commands her to rise from her low couch. She removes the bandages on her arms and gets up. She thanks Jesus—as do all who are present. When a meal is served, the mother-in-law completely well, helps serve (ACE 2 263).

Another reading given by Edgar Cayce (2358-1) tells the recipient that she is, in a previous life, Peter's mother-in-law and refers to the illness with the fever. In conclusion, Cayce in trance suggests that her life reading would be quite interesting, but the thirty-eight-year-old woman does not make the request.

Another holy woman who is not mentioned before receives the following readings from Edgar Cayce:

> The entity was among those families in Bethsaida; in which the entity made the home His resting place. Hence the entity was close to and acquainted with Him; and gave self even in physical activities for the pleasure, the comfort of a tired man—the Son of God. We find the entity became close in its activity with those who were the establishers of the church; among the holy women, and a helper oft. For, the entity was young in years during those periods of contact with Him in the physical manner; yet those periods, those activities, those conscious moments in His presence, with those happenings that to the entity were the loss not only of a friend but of a Savior, brought awe-inspiring experiences in the mental and the spiritual self that are a part of that consciousness experienced by many in the present who come into the very presence of the entity, though the entity is now not so oft conscious of such in the physical consciousness of the entity.
>
> The name then was Morao. Too much might not be said as to the attainments of the entity through that experience, and as to the activities in a helpful manner that the entity brought into the experiences even of the closer disciples in their periods of disturbance because of physical conditions.   1223-4

And in a subsequent reading:

> The entity, as indicated, was in the teen-age years when
> first becoming acquainted with the tenets and teachings
> of the Master. The entity was an acquaintance of Peter,
> Andrew, James and John. Because of the entity's parent,
> the father being associated with those in their activities
> upon the sea in those relationships then, the entity was
> acquainted with Peter's mother-in-law who was healed in
> the early ministry of the Master. Oft the entity sought to
> make the things, the conditions, more comfortable for the
> Master; and thus may it be said that the entity became so
> closely associated with Jesus as to call Him by His name,
> Jesus, not Master until after His crucifixion . . . The entity
> was known among the holy women, even to a great age.
> Married, yes, during those experiences, to one Turteltus of
> the Roman peoples.   1223-9

Other people receive readings telling them they observed the healing of Peter's mother-in-law. One such reading is for Josie:

> The entity was among those of Peter's household, and one
> that was called when Peter's mother-in-law was healed. In
> the experience the entity suffered physically, yet in its in-
> ner self there were the desires for might and power and
> physical ability to meet emergencies. There was that de-
> termination (though delicate in the body as in the present)
> which brought the experience of the stalwart Bruce; who
> found that "It is not by might nor by power, but by my
> spirit, saith the Lord of hosts."
> The entity had acquaintanceships with all of those who
> led in the many ways of activity, both pro and con in the
> experience. For the entity saw much, hoped for much, and
> yet felt in self that it was accomplishing so little. It prayed
> oft for a physical body to meet physical conditions.
> The name then was Josie, and of those who saw not
> only the beginning of the miracles but the mightiest one of

> all—the cross, the tomb and the resurrection, which once
> gathered in and becoming a part of the soul may never be
> lost   2448-2

Another observer is Ruth, sister of Jesus who is told, "In life ye saw
Him, in experience and manifestations as when He healed Peter's wife's
mother, just before the rising of the rulers of the temple against Him."
(1158-9)

Other events taking place some time after the healing of Peter's
mother-in-law involve relatives of Peter and his wife. Jesus sends Peter,
Andrew, and John to meet about ten holy women at an inn near Jericho. Among these women are Mother Mary, Martha, Magdalen, Peter's
wife and step-daughter, Andrew's wife, and Zacheus's wife and daughter (ACE 3 582). This is one of the few times we hear of Andrew's wife.
Another time the holy women leave Peter's house and go to Andrew's
house at the north end of Bethsaida. At the same time, Jesus takes
Saturnin and another disciple and goes to a hospital very close to
Andrew's house. The hospital houses lepers, those possessed, and other
pitiful, forlorn cases. Jesus has the superintendent bring these people
out into the court. Then Jesus goes about counseling, comforting, and
healing while the disciples give them clothing brought especially for
that purpose. These forgotten people cry and thank Jesus and His disciples. Then they take the superintendent to Andrew's house to dine.
Andrew serves them a very fine fish dinner. His wife is an energetic,
active person, who seldom leaves the house. She employs many poor
girls in fish net weaving. She has a very orderly business and welcomes
fallen, repudiated wives as they are turned out with no place to go.
Andrew's wife gives them work, instructs them in their duty and in how
to implore God's mercy (ACE 2 223-225).

There is another important relative of Peter and his mother-in-law.
She is Martha, the sister of Peter's mother-in-law. According to Cayce:

> The entity was acquainted with the Master, being a sister
> of Peter's wife's mother. Thus the entity was acquainted
> with the first of the outward miracles of healing in that ex-

perience, and has looked for and may find in its own hands
the abilities to heal others in His name. Not of self but in
His name.

In the experience the entity ever remained through the
period one of those of the holy women. The timidity, the
backwardness, and yet the exaltation that may be the experience of many by merely being in the presence of the
entity, arises from that sojourn. For, as has been indicated
all feel a variation, a difference, by the very presence of the
entity in any company. This is not to be used other than as
given; kindness, gentleness, patience, persistence and
brotherly love. These are the fruits of the spirit. These ye
then made manifest. These ye may again make manifest.
There, too, the entity made for much color, and it was this
entity that prepared the robe of one piece for the Master.
The name then was Martha.   3175-1

Another much longer reading addresses the life of Martha saying:

Yes, the entity's experience in the earth plane as Martha.
The sister of Peter's wife's mother. Yes, we are again given
the records here of that entity . . . A lovely body!

In giving the experiences of the entity in the earth plane
as Martha, the sister of Peter's wife's mother, it would be
well that much of the happenings or history of the times be
included, that there may be the more perfect understanding of the conditions and as to how and why urges from
that experience apply in the present.

As is understood by many, there had been long a looking forward to or for the advent of the promised Messiah
into the earth and there had been those various groups
through one channel or another who had banded together
to study the material which was handed down through the
varied groups in that day and period.

Here we find there had been, for the mother of Martha,
an experience of coming in touch with Judy [1472] who
had been the first of women appointed as the head of the
Essenes group who had the experience of having voices,

as well as those which would be called in the present experiences communications with the influences which had
been a part of man's experience from the beginning, such
that the divine within man heard the experiences of those
forces outside of man and communicated in voices, in
dreams, in signs and symbols which had become a portion
of the experience.

When the children of Martha's mother, Sophia, were in
those periods of development these had become a part of
what would be called today a play-experience for the entity, Martha.

For Peter's wife's mother was many years the senior of
Martha but the coming of John, and the birth of Jesus, the
dispensation of Jesus and John in Egypt, all had an impression or imprint upon the mind of the entity Martha, who
builded in her own mind how the king and how the an-
nouncer of the king should be dressed, (as this had been a
part of the experiences of the entity in other periods and
thus the choice of things in this direction).

Then there came those great changes in the life experience of Martha. For one among those of the rulers of the
synagogue sought the entity in marriage and through the
individuals who made these arrangements the entity was
espoused to Nicodemus [3021]. Through his activities, and
personality, Martha learned first of what had happened to
the peoples in the homes of John the Baptist and of Mary
and Joseph and Jesus.

Thus, when there were later the experiences of those
entering into activities, and then when the message was
given out that Martha's older sister had been healed from
a terrible fever by this man, Jesus, this brought about great
changes in Nicodemus and Martha, as they had to do with
the temple and the service of the high priest. Martha began the weaving of the robe that became as a part of the
equipment the Master had. Thus the robe was made especially for the Master. In color it was not as the robe of the
priest, but woven in the one piece with the hole in the top
through which the head was to be placed, and then over

the body, so that with the cords it was bound about the waist.

This robe Nicodemus presented then to the Master, Jesus, after the healing of the widow of Nain's son, who was a relative of Nicodemus.

In the activities, then, when Nicodemus went to the Master by night and there became those discussions in the home, for Nicodemus and Martha there began the communion as man and wife rather than man and his chattel or his servant. They were more on a basis of equality, not in the same proportions which were established a bit later by some of the rulers from the Roman land but more in keeping with the happenings which had brought about the activities in the Essenes group.

Though Martha was an Essene, Nicodemus never accepted completely the tenets of the teachings of the Essenes group. These were a part of the principles and applications of Martha. The acquaintanceships, the friendships which were established between Mary, Elizabeth and the other Mary [2946], all were parts of the experience and because of the position of Martha throughout those activities she was considered rather one of the leaders, or one to whom others made appeal to have positions or conditions set in motion so that there was given more concessions to the Holy Women who followed Jesus from place to place when there were those periods of His Palestine ministry.

The only differences which arose were with Martha and Mary in the household of Lazarus, Martha and Mary. Because of conditions there from which Mary had returned, from the houses which were a portion of her activity in various cities, questions as to morality arose. And yet, after there were the healings, or as it was discovered how she out of whom seven devils were cast became changed, or how there were even changes then and there, we find there was a greater working together with the activities of Mary, Martha, Lazarus and Mary the mother of Jesus, Elijah and many of those others, including John Mark's mother. These were parts of the experience of the entity. The entity stood, as indicated by the accomplishments of the robe from Nicodemus, as one particularly honored even by the Master.

During the periods of activity, during the missions after the Crucifixion and Resurrection of the Master, the entity Martha gathered with those in the upper room looking for the promise of the coming of the outpouring of the Holy Spirit. This, too, became a part of the activities. For the entity later was among those who aided Stephen and Philip, as well as others of the various lands. For it was with these that the entity first became acquainted with Luke and Lucius who later became the heads of various organizations in other portions. These acquaintances were then rather as counsel from those to whom Luke, Lucius, Mark as the younger of the Disciples, (not Apostles, but younger of the Disciples), went for counsel. For the entity was one acquainted with the law, the entity Martha, taught the law to the young ones, the children who sought knowledge.

The entity had its own family, two sons and one daughter. These became ministers in the church in Antioch, aiding the peoples who worked with Barnabas, and it is mentioned that one, Theopolus learned from the entity Sylvanus, and those who labored in the church in Jerusalem with John, James, Peter and the others, as a child. As a child, this one was known as Thaddeus. The daughter was wed to one of the companions of Paul, Silas [707], who was engaged in a portion of the activities with Paul . . .

The entity lived to be an elderly person, something like seventy-nine years of age in the experience, and was not among those ever beaten or placed in jail, though persecuted by only the Romans, feared by those of her own peoples.   3175-3

Martha is present at the crucifixion. After the resurrection people pour into Bethany and Jerusalem, and the disciples and holy women help the newcomers settle into the Community. Many dwell in tents, including Peter's wife and daughter, Mark's wife, and many other women coming to Bethany from Bethsaida. They live separately from the men and are with the Apostles only for instruction. They involve themselves in weaving, embroidery, and working on creating tents. The holy women, who include Zacheus's wife, share with the new women coming in. No one owns anything. Those with much give up much. Nicodemus, Joseph of Arimathea, Magdalen, Martha, and Lazarus turn their houses over to the new converts. Those who have little receive what they need (ACE 4 417).

Chapter 13

Other Holy Women from the Cayce Readings

There is a wider range and time period for women termed "holy women" in the Cayce readings than in the nun's visions. Here are a number of these readings to illustrate the point and demonstrate the considerable diversity of backgrounds of these women and pathways to the designation of holy woman.

Judy is a very important figure as sections from two of her readings will show:

> The entity was in the Palestine land, during those days when the Master walked in the earth; and when there were the peoples about those activities of not only the birth but His sojourns before and after the return from Egypt—those whom Judy blessed, that labored in the preserving of the records of *His* activities as the child; the activities of the Wise Men, the Essenes and the groups to which Judy had been the prophetess, the healer, the writer, the recorder— for all of these groups.
>
> And though questioned or scoffed at by the Roman rulers and the tax gatherers, and especially those that made

for the levying or the providing for those activities for the taxation, the entity gained throughout. Though the heart and body was often weary from the toils of the day, and the very imprudence—yea, the very selfishness of others for the aggrandizing of their bodies rather than their souls or minds seeking development, the entity grew in grace, in knowledge, in understanding.   1472-1

In the third reading for Judy, Cayce explains that she:

Seeks detailed information concerning her Palestine sojourn as Judy, covering her biographical life, work and associations throughout that experience, from the entity's entrance to her departure.

Here we may give even portions of the records as scribed by the entity called Judy, as the teacher, as the healer, as the prophetess through that experience.

Some four and twenty years before the advent of that entity, that soul-entrance into material plane called Jesus, we find Phinehas and Elkatma making those activities among those of the depleted group of the prophets in Mt Carmel; that begun by Samuel, Elisha, Elijah, Saul, and those during those early experiences.

Because of the divisions that had arisen among the peoples into sects, as the Pharisee, the Sadducee and their divisions, there had arisen the Essenes that had cherished not merely the conditions that had come as word of mouth but had kept the records of the periods when individuals had been visited with the supernatural or out of the ordinary experiences; whether in dreams, visions, voices, or what not that had been and were felt by these students of the customs, of the law, of the activities throughout the experiences of this peculiar people—the promises and the many ways these had been interpreted by those to whom the preservation of same had been committed. Hence we find Phinehas and the companion, both having received the experience similar to that received by Hannah and Elkanah, had drawn aside from many of the other groups. And then as in answer to that promise, the child—Judy—was born. That the entity was a daughter, rather than being a male, brought some disturbance, some confusion in the minds of many.

Yet the life, the experiences of the parents had been such that still—fulfilling their promise—they brought the life of their child, Judy, and dedicated it to the study and the application of self to the study of those things that had been handed down as a part of the *experiences* of those who had received visitations from the unseen, the un-known—or that worshiped as the Divine Spirit moving into the activities of man.

Hence we find the entity Judy was brought up in that environment; not of disputations, not of argumentations, but rather as that of rote and writ—as was considered necessary for the development, the influences, the activi-ties of the life, to induce or to bring about those experi-ences. That much had been to that period as tradition rather than as record, appeared—from the activity of the entity, Judy—to have made a great impression. So there was the setting about to seek means and manners for the preservation, and for the making of records of that which had been handed down as word of mouth, as tradition. Such channels and ways were sought out. And eventually the manner was chosen in which records were being kept in Egypt rather than in Persia, from which much of the tra-dition arose—of course—because of the very indwelling of the peoples in that land. Hence not only the manners of the recording but also the traditions of Egypt, the tradi-tions from India, the conditions and traditions from many of the Persian lands and from many of the borders about same, became a part of the studies and the seeking of the entity Judy early in the attempts to make, keep and pre-serve such records.

The manners of communication being adverse, owing to the political situations that gradually arose due to the Ro-man influence in the land, made more and more a recluse of the entity in the early periods; until there were those visitations by what ye call the Wise Men of the East—one from Persia, one from India, one from the Egyptian land. These reasoned with the Brethren, but more was sought from the studies of the entity Judy at that experience. Then there was the report by the Wise Men to the king. Has it been thought of, or have you heard it reasoned as to why the Wise Men went to Herod, who was only second or third in authority rather than to the Romans who were *all* authority in the land? Because of Judy; knowing that this would arouse in the heart and mind of this debased ruler—that only sought for the aggrandizement of self—such reactions as to bring to him, this despot, turmoils with those then in authority. Why? There was not the proclamation by the Wise Men, neither by Judy nor the Essenes, that this new king was to replace Rome! It was to replace the Jewish authority in the land!

Thus we find, as it would be termed in the present, attention was called or pointed to the activity of the Essenes such that a little later—during those periods of the sojourn of the Child in Egypt because of same—Herod issues the edict for the destruction. This brought to those that were close to the entity those periods that were best described by the entity itself, in the cry of Rachel for her children that were being born into a period of opportunity—yet the destructive forces, by the very edict of this tyrant, made them as naught.

Hence during those periods of the ministry of John, and then of Jesus, more and more questioning was brought upon the recorder—or Judy—by the Roman authorities, or the Roman spies, or those who were the directors of those who collected and who registered taxes of those peoples for the Roman collection. Consequently, we find the entity came in contact with the Medes, the Persians, the Indian influence of authority—because of the commercial association as well as the influence that had been upon the world by those activities of Sanoid and those that were known during the periods of Brahma and Buddha. These brought to the experience of the entity the weighing of the counsels from the traditions of the Egyptians and of her own kind—and then that new understanding.

Hence we find the entity in those periods soon after the Crucifixion not only giving comfort but a better interpretation to the Twelve, to the Holy Women; an understanding as to how Woman was redeemed from a place of obscurity to her place in the activities of the affairs of the race, of the world, of the empire—yea, of the home itself. Those all became a part of the entity's experiences during that portion.

Hence we find many have been, many are, the contacts the entity has made and must make in this present experience. For, as then, the evolution of man's experiences is for the individual purpose of becoming more and more acquainted with those activities in the relationships with the fellow man, as an exemplification, as a manifestation of Divine Love—as was shown by the Son of man, Jesus; that *each* and every soul *must become, must be* the *Savior* of some soul! To even *comprehend* the purpose of the entrance of the Son *into* the earth—that man might have the closer walk with, yea the open door to, the very heart of the living God!

The entity's activities during the persecutions aroused much in the minds of those that made war again and again upon the followers of the Nazarene, of Jesus, of the Apostles here and there. And the entity, as would be termed, was hounded, yea was persecuted the more and more; yet remaining until what ye would call the sixty-seventh year *after* the Crucifixion; or until Time itself began to be counted from same. For the records as were borne by the entity, it will be found, were *begun* by the activities of the entity during what ye would term a period sixty years *after* the crucifixion. And then they were reckoned first by the peoples of Carmel, and then by the brethren in Antioch, then a portion of Jerusalem, then to Smyrna, Philadelphia, and those places where these were becoming more active.

The entity—though receiving rebuffs, yea even stripes in the body—died a natural death in that experience; at

the age then of ninety-one. . . .
(Q) How close was my association with Jesus in my Palestine sojourn?
(A) A portion of the experience the entity was the teacher! How close? So close that the very heart and purposes were proclaimed of those things that were traditions! For the entity sent Him to Persia, to Egypt, yea to India, that there might be completed the more perfect knowledge of the material ways in the activities of Him that became the Way, the Truth!   1472-3

The reader may at this point ask the same question asked by the entity:

(Q) If, as you have said, I was a prophetess, healer, teacher and writer in my Palestine sojourn, why does so-called sacred history give no record of me or my work?
(A) Ye were of the Essenes; not of the Jews nor even the Samaritans!   1472-6

Another question the reader may want answered is why Judy was not a boy as the parents expected. The answer given is:

That is from the powers on high, and gave the first demonstration of woman's place in the affairs and associations of man. For, as were the teachings of Jesus, that released woman from that bondage to which she had been held since the ideas of man conceived from the fall of Eve, or of her first acceptance of the opinions—these were the first, and those activities that brought about, in the teachings materially, that as Jesus proclaimed.   2067-11

Other interesting comments regarding Judy in this same reading tell us that she was Jesus' teacher for five years. She had a husband and a son. She was not physically present at the crucifixion, but she was there in spirit and mind as she was capable of being present without the presence of her physical body.

When Philoas, the Roman husband of Ruth, the sister of Jesus, asks what his relationship was with Judy, the answer comes:

> Just as would be intimated—as here the entity Judy was held in reverence by all of the followers of Jesus, though persecuted oft by the Jews—or the sects of the Jews— under various circumstances. But not as an informer was the entity considered by the entity now known as [1151], but as one that would and that did give the facts of the activities of various groups in respect to not only the Essenes but the other portions of the various groups in the land. The association then was quite close at times, at others not so closely associated yet keeping in touch with the activities.   1151-10

As the first woman to head the Essenes, a teacher of Jesus, and a highly advanced spiritual person, Judy deserves the title holy woman without question.

Jesus often visited Bethsaida. Some of the holy women resided there and welcomed Jesus and His disciples.

Cayce mentioned the woman named Leah, saying she:

> . . . was then among those coming under the influence of the Master through those teachings especially in Bethsaida. Then the entity was associated with those activities about the disciples and their sojourns in that land, and later became one of the holy women that aided in the establishing of homes for those that were questioned as to their associations with the groups who came as rulers—or as the soldiery in that land. Thus the entity became one upon whom many relied for counsel.   2960-1

Matildah is another holy woman from Bethsaida. About her Cayce says:

> The entity was among those who saw many of the experiences that brought the awareness of the unusualness and

the divinity of the Master; being present at the feeding of the five thousand, also when there were those wonderments at His joining His disciples without means of transportation in the ship; also present when there were the relatings of the happenings to the men when the evil forces were driven from same—and the destruction of the hogs.

These made, then, those activities in which the entity gained. For, the entity was among those who might truly be called the holy women, yet not among those in the disturbance in Jerusalem—but was there on the day of Pentecost.   2845-2

A Cayce reading for Morao says:

The entity was among those families in Bethsaida; in which the entity made the home His resting place. Hence the entity was close to and acquainted with Him; and gave self even in physical activities for the pleasure, the comfort, of a tired man—the son of god.

We find that the entity became close in its activity with those who were the establishers of the church; among the holy women, and a helper oft. For, the entity was young in years during those periods of contact with Him in the physical manner; yet those periods, those activities, those conscious moments in His presence, with those happenings that to the entity were the loss not only of a friend but of a Savior, brought awe inspiring experiences in the mental and the spiritual self that are a part of that consciousness experienced by many in the present who come into the very presence of the entity; though the entity is now not so oft conscious of such in the physical consciousness of the entity. But in moments of deep meditation and prayer, there comes oft that vision as of seeing His face—worn at times; at others that smile, that expression that brings the hope so necessary in the heart of the human—that there *is* the better way, there is safety in His presence, in the consciousness of the abiding faith in Him.

The name then was Morao. Too much might not be said

as to the attainments of the entity through that experience,
and as to the activities in a helpful manner that the entity
brought into the experiences even of the closer disciples
in their periods of disturbance because of physical conditions.   1223-4

More information comes in a later reading for Morao:

Bethsaida was among the places often visited by the Master, as it was among the peoples of this place where the
Master liked to rest.

The entity was in the teen-age years when first becoming acquainted with the tenets and teachings of the Master. The entity was an acquaintance of Peter, Andrew,
James and John. Because of the entity's parent, the father
being associated with those in their activities upon the sea
in those relationships then, the entity was acquainted with
Peter's mother-in-law who was healed in the early ministry
of the Master. And during the Master's sojourning in
Bethsaida in the periods when He preached by the sea-
shore, as well as when He rested, the entity knew of and
was acquainted personally with the Master. Oft the entity
sought to make the things, the conditions, more comfortable for the Master; and thus may it be said that the entity
became so closely associated with Jesus as to call Him by
His name, Jesus, not Master until after His crucifixion.

In the experiences the entity not only then talked with
but questioned the Master; and thus those tenets, the
teachings that the Master gave as to friendships, associations, forgiveness, the lack of common gossip about others, were those warnings which were a portion of the
experience with Jesus of Nazareth by the entity, Morao.

So, when there came about those periods when the Disciples were scattered because of the happenings in Jerusalem after the Resurrection, the entity was known as one
who would aid, did aid in the ministering to the needs of
the ministers, preachers or saints, as they are commonly
termed, who were the active ones in the Christian ministry

after His Resurrection. Thus the entity became so imbued
with those tenets, those teachings, that little may be said
as to how great were the ideals, how great was the love of
the entity for those ideals. How great the desire and purpose of the entity in telling the stories of, encouraging others by, those direct experiences the entity had with the
Master. . .

The entity was known among the Holy Women, even to
a great age. Married, yes, during those experiences, to one
Turteltus of the Roman peoples.   1223-9

The wives of the Apostles are rarely introduced so that they become
independent identities. One reading introduces the wife of Thomas. Her
name is Jose. She is referred to as "a helpmate to Mary, the mother of
the Lord." Jose helped during Jesus' childhood when the family returned
from Egypt. These activities greatly influence her life even in the present
lifetime. She has times of fear and doubt but for others and not herself.
She is acquainted with a great many of the followers of Jesus, and becomes the wife of Thomas (2037-1).

Julia, a holy woman, is of Thomas' household. She is active when
"the man of Galilee" receives praise and also during the period of dis-
agreements and separation sorrows. She is present at Jesus' ascension.
Her experiences still serve her because she trusts the promises in spite
of Thomas' doubting.

As Julia she strengthens others' faith and hope, and she continues to
do the same presently because of the strong influence of Jesus. She
agrees with the concept of to be a servant of all is to hold the greatest
position (2272-1).

Cayce gives a reading for Sofa, one referred to as a holy woman. She
lives a life involved with the family of Zachariah, Elizabeth, and John.

She was in the Promised Land, during those periods when
there was the looking for, and the expectancy of the
peoples for the fulfilling of the promises which had been a
part of the Scripture, as well as a part of the things that

were hearsay. The entity was closely associated with the mother of the forerunner of the Master—and the entity made itself, by choice, the nurse of John.

Thus the message of John—"Prepare ye the way, the day of the Lord is at hand!"—is a part of the entity's seal of life, as we have indicated in the Arabic inscription on the ribbon.

Then the entity was in the name Sofa, and gained; though at times very discouraged at the happenings and misunderstandings of those peoples because of the inabilities to know of the teachings of the Master as well as of John.

And when there were those days of persecution and imprisonment, the entity suffered—in body, in mind.

Thus the songs and the Psalms become as the tenets or truths that are the manners and means in which the entity may find expression—as from the lyre or harp in the seal of the entity's life.   2175-1

A later reading for Sofa adds:

Zachariah was a just man, then living in the hills of Galilee; yet the priest who offered sacrifice for the month Nisan. And when there were those visions or experiences, and his wife Elizabeth conceived, these brought into the experience of those groups—of which this entity, Sofa, was a part—the Essenes—a great deal of questioning—as to what manner of individual would be required or needed as the helper, or director, or nurse, in the circumstances that would naturally arise if these visions were to be fulfilled.

When there has been the experience, then, of the happening of the visit of Mary to Elizabeth, there was the choosing of the dedicated women for this office. This was a reminder to many of what and how the maiden had been chosen on the stair.

The entity then, Sofa, was one of the women dedicated to service in the temple; not as one that would be called a caretaker, yet these were the offices of the entity—to "touch up" or paint, or to keep certain portions of the temple in order for the activities of the priest. Thus the entity appealed to Zachariah to use his period of preparation as the one to offer sacrifice, as the time when there would be the choosing of the attendant or nurse to the babe. Hence the entity was chosen by what would be termed, or is termed in the Cabala, the moving of the symbols upon the vesture of the priest. This, then, prevented *any* of those confusions as might have arisen with the entity.

When there was the birth, then, of John (for, remember, he was not called the Baptist until after his death), in the periods of training, the entity also acted as the instructor; as in the position of one who looks after or cares for those through such periods. And (this aside), too often there is not sufficient thought taken as to the care of a developing body through those first eighteen months to two years.

Here, though, this entity was chosen by those directing forces as from the temple service itself, or by divine guidance. Thus did the entity fulfill, until the boy, John, was weaned at six years of age.

Then the entity was associated with Jesus with the last year of the experience in the household of Mary and Joseph. While the offices here had been fulfilled by that one as we have indicated, the entity was especially given this office to indicate to the developing child the nature, the character of the cousin.

After that period, and the period of education, and the periods when the labor began—from the periods of twelve years to that of seventeen—when the entity John went to Egypt for the dedication and the preparation there—the entity was known among those who were as holy women, who acted in the capacity of the mourners at the various functions of the Order, as would be called, of the Essenes.

Later the entity was among those, not *the* first but *among* the first, to be baptized by John in Jordan.

The entity also ministered to the needs of John when he was cast in prison, and was among the chief mourners when he was beheaded. The entity also was among those who, during his period in prison, sought Jesus for counsel. And with the answers given, the entity was confused—until there were those reclaiming activities upon the day of Pentecost.

Then the entity was old in years, and among those first disturbed by the first edicts that brought death to James; the entity dying in that period from exposure by the abuse of soldiers in that first raid . . .

As to the entity's parents—these were of the Levites, and those acquainted with many of the activities in the temple. And from same, ceremony means much to the entity. Whatever the preparation, for whatever function, to the entity there must be some ceremony.   2175-6

In the question and answer section of the reading, the woman asks about the relatives of Sofa. Cayce tells her that Sister Duene (2308) is a younger sister of Sofa. It is not clear if Sister Duene is actually a holy woman, but her reading is interesting and gives more insight as to the services of the later holy women.

The entity was in the land of promise, during those periods when there were the holy women set as the heads of the church, or as counselors; not as deaconesses, not as those today considered as sisters of mercy or sisters superior, but rather those who took the veil that there might be the better preparations of self to be offered as channels through which greater blessings might come, and greater abilities for teaching. They were those who separated themselves from their families, their homes that they might become as channels of blessings to others.

The entity was known then as Sister Duene. In the experience the entity gained throughout, through the abilities as a nurse, as a teacher, as a reader, as a song giver, as one who read poetry. For, the entity was acquainted with many of those called the saints of the church, as the entity was acquainted with the Master Himself.   2308-1

The recipient of the Sofa reading also asks if she, as Sofa, associated with Lucius. Cayce says she served as an advisor to him (2175–6).

Then, there is a reading for Merceden, the mother of Lucius (2574). She travels to lands involved with Greek activities. As a sister of Luke, she works with the holy women. Her children are influenced by the teachings of both Jesus and His disciples.

Merceden helps bring harmony to the conflict arising among followers of Paul, Peter, and Barnabas while Lucius is a church bishop. She also develops activities that early churches, especially in Laodicea, Achaia, and Corinth adopt.

The recipient of the reading hears: "One need never attempt to justify, but needs only to glorify Him; as ye so well proclaimed through Laodicea, as ye so well put Paul in his place, as ye so well comforted Timothy as well as Peter and Andrew, and brought Lucius to his senses." (2574–1)

The variety of backgrounds of holy women is surprisingly well shown in the readings of the following two women: Cleopeo and Beatrice.

> Cleopeo lived in the earth during the days when the Master walked therein, especially in that period just previous to His teachings that became as the examples to all— through not only the material benefits for the secular life but those that made for the answering to that longing that arises ever within the human breast for the continuation of a consciousness that will live on and on.
>
> The entity then was among the entertainers at the court of Herod. And if the entity will read oft the record of the dance of those that asked for the head of John the Baptist, there will come—with meditations—a feeling of emotions that may not be aroused by any other sort of experience.
>
> Yet when those of that court came under the influence of the teachings of the Master, when there were the healings of Pontius Pilate's son by the Master, the entity then joined with those that are rather later spoken of as the holy women—that followed afar, yea and made for many preparations for those that were to come under the

persecutions of those in the latter days.

The entity then, in the name Cleopeo, gained through-out; for those experiences in pomp and power, in the lowly walks among the needy, the persecuted, brought for the entity an inner feeling that should be kept even as the light burning within the heart ever, that may make for that as its ideal in all of its experiences in the present, even as it in the former appearances and experience held to the Law of One which was exemplified as the same through those teachings given by Him who was to the entity the friend and the Savior.   1207-1

Cayce says that the entity's life as Beatrice is as follows:

She was in what is now called the Holy Land, during those periods when there were the questionings as to the sol-diery from the Roman rule, when there were the questionings of the teacher John.

The entity then was in the capacity of being among those who furnished entertainment, as a danseuse for Herod. And the entity was in close associations then with those under that individual's activity, and with those not only of Pilate's court but of the Roman associations; also with those that furnished the emperor's activities in the changes that were wrought.

Those experiences brought spectacular activities in the experiences of the entity; though losing oft in the experi-ences, because of self-indulgences, self's gratifications.

With those periods when there was the harkening to those that joined in what was afterward termed in the records as the triumphal entry of the man of Galilee, a change came into the experience of the entity. And joining with many of those that were numbered among the holy women, the entity's activities then brought forth a service to many of many lands.

For as there were gathered those from all the lands for the periods of that particular feast when the entity became overcome, as it were, by the bodily abuses in many direc-

> tions during the period, the *healing* that was accomplished
> not only by the words spoken but by the look, by the touch
> of the Holy One, brought joy and glory and understanding
> and knowledge and *wisdom* to the experience of the en-
> tity.
> Then, as Beatrice, who helped in the preparations of the
> linens about the head of the Master when entombed by
> Josephus [Greek-Latin form of Joseph] [Joseph of Arimathea]
> and the friends, the entity gained; for it gave of self, it
> brought aid and help.   1081-1

One woman's reading tells her that she is in the Holy Land as a
Roman of the upper class at the time of Jesus. She is present at the trial
and the crucifixion of Jesus. When Jesus arises the third day, Amorela
(her name then) joins the holy women.

At the trial before Pilate, Amorela sees Jesus' face and the tenderness
He displays when followers desert Him. The Master speaks to her, "Be
not afraid, for me nor for thy self. *All* is *well* with thee."

Amorela attempts to learn the truth of the resurrection, and, consequently, weeps much.

The reading advises her to know that Jesus heals, and give Him credit
for her abilities as well as giving Him love and honor.

Finally, the reading reminds her to keep the commandments, which
she is doing, and to preserve, live, and be them (2620-2).

Elenor is another who lives during the time of Herod. People are
fearful and questioning because of edicts from a ruler cause children to
be murdered. Although there is peace politically, a great number of
people losing their little ones have no peace but only turmoil, strife,
and sorrow.

Elenor hears the mothers and fathers speak of their murdered chil-
dren and gradually seeks to learn the background of Herod's edicts.
She, therefore, becomes acquainted with the mysteries surrounding
Zachariah, Mary and Joseph's journey to and return from Egypt.

She becomes a companion to the followers of the Master and learns
His teachings. It appeals to her that Jesus teaches being kind, helping
others, and bringing hope, cheer, and joy. By doing these things and

having faith in Him, "He will bear thee up."

As Elenor applies these teachings in her work with the holy women, Mother Mary, and all those she meets, as the persecutions begins, she well comprehends, "The day of the Lord is at hand." (2400-1)

Hired mourners are part of the culture of the time. Some of these women are involved in that capacity at the death of Lazarus and become holy women. Martia is one in this group. About Martia, Cayce says:

> The entity was in the earth when the Master walked in the land, among those that were of the holy women. In the beginning the entity was among that group of hired mourners at the passing of Lazarus. Becoming acquainted with the Master there, having the closer association with Mary, Martha, Lazarus, John, James, the other Mary, and Mary the Mother after the Crucifixion, brought the entity close to those activities that made the entity ever as one to whom many came for counsel. Many rely upon just being in the presence of the entity, that they might gain something from those activities, those words that the entity gives expression to. Yet the entity is active in many realms of activities, as it was in that experience in the name Martia.
>
> 3954-1

Another hired mourner named Ruhel appears in the following reading:

> For, during the period when the Master walked in the earth, the entity was a hired mourner. At those periods when Lazarus was raised from the tomb the entity came in contact with and knew the presence of the Master Himself.
>
> This is the gift of the entity in preparation of the home; not so much of self as for others, in making a home for those on special missions in their experience in the earth.
>
> The name then was Ruhel. The entity became acquainted with the Holy Women, during those periods preceding and following the Crucifixion, when the entity was

drawn closer to the mother of Zebedee's children and the other Mary.

These brought an experience that has been and will be far-reaching in the earth, as to the conviction that lies deep in the heart as to the voice within. Hold to same. For, He has ever promised, "I stand and knock—open, and I will enter." Ye must open, ye must desire, ye must wish for, ye must try; and He will do His part. Seek not to do His part but do thine own.   3179-1

Sobol is another hired mourner and holy woman. Cayce says of her:

She was in the Promised Land, during those periods when the Master walked in the earth; when there were those experiences in the city of Bethany. The entity was among those of the acquaintances, though acted in the capacity as a hired mourner at the death and burial, of Lazarus.

There the entity became acquainted with those two vital forces of such different natures—Mary and Martha. Most of all the entity knew Jesus, and reminded even John that He wept as He spoke to Martha respecting the resurrection.

The entity witnessed the resurrection of Lazarus, the calling forth from the tomb, and was present and an aid at the great feast given to the friends and to Jesus and His disciples. And from that day forth the entity was among those called the Holy Women; becoming only acquainted with the Mother of Jesus after the day of the Crucifixion, when there had been that injunction, "Behold thy son. Behold thy mother."

These brought those experiences in the innate forces of this entity, so that mother and son—even the expression—brings a vibration to the entity not felt by many; brings a welling up of emotion as experienced only by those whose names are written in the book of life or—as He called—in heaven . . . The name then was Sobol.   2787-1

Thelda is in the Palestine land at the time of Jesus and is a hired mourner when Lazarus dies. Cayce remarks:

> There we find the entity was among those who were the acquaintances of Martha and Mary, to whom the Master came oft. The entity was among those who were the hired ones as a mourner at the time of Lazarus' death; and became a believer—seeing the activities, experiencing the influence of the Master's life on the friends, associates and acquaintances of that group there. And from henceforth the entity was known as one among those of the holy women.
>
> Then the name was Thelda, and in the experience the entity gained. While it was late in years (according to the years of many of those women of that experience) when the entity became acquainted with all of the activities of the disciples, all of the apostles, all of the influences brought about during those periods just before and after the Crucifixion were experienced by the entity.
>
> The entity also saw that experience of the Crucifixion— the darkening of the day, the rending of the veil of the temple, the noises that were experienced—as well as those periods that followed same, in the upper room, when the entity with the followers of the Master was made aware of His resurrection. For those things that happened to the peoples and children of the entity's acquaintances were witnessed, as well as to the heathen—or especially the Romans.
>
> There we find the entity was closely associated with Mariaerh [1468], who was the companion of Lucius in the activities in Laodicea. For the entity then was the aunt of that entity, bringing her into close associations with the activities of the people in that experience.
>
> Throughout the entity gained, for those tenets—as well as desires and purposes and intents—became deep-seated within the soul of the entity; and these oft rise within the experience.   1986-1

Thelda's niece Mariaerh may not have been an official member of the holy women, but she received readings that associate her with the holy women, and her life is worthy of inclusion with this group of women. Cayce says:

> During those sojourns of the individuals from many portions of the Judean land, the entity was then among those peoples of the hill country that came to the city during those periods of feast—when there was the triumphal entry into Jerusalem. The entity for the first time then saw (though it had heard of) the activities of the man called Jesu, or Jesus, in those experiences.
>
> And when there were the cries of "Hosanna!" and there were the processions, these brought strange feelings to the entity, as a harking to something that had lain dormant within the experiences of self—and the wonder became rather that of a worshipfulness. *Then* the entity, as Mariaerh, made overtures; joining with those for the searching out of those activities of that strange new experience of self.
>
> And the entity in those periods became among those that ministered to needs of those that were supplied by the gifts of those during the days following the persecutions and the establishing of the church, or the groups in the various portions of the city.
>
> The entity grew in years and joined with the activities, for it was only in its teens when these began; and the entity was from the upper portion of the Judean land.
>
> 1468-1

Cayce makes a stronger connection between Mariaerh and the holy women in a second reading:

> Hence we find the entity was an early acquaintance with many of those that were associated during those periods, as were later called the Holy Women—that stood about the sepulchre, about the Cross, that made preparations for the burial or the activities regarding same. . .
>
> As to the entity's experience after same, we find there

soon followed the historical events of the arrest, the trial and the Crucifixion; and those days followed—and then those periods when the entity remained in and about Bethany and the areas about same.

Then, fifty days later when there was again the Pentecostal activity, when all of the gatherings were in Jerusalem and there were the many of many lands and of many tongues that were brought to conviction by the teachings of the disciples or Apostles, and especially in that memorial one of Peter's on the day of Pentecost, we find the entity was among the first ten that were baptized on that day.

Then when there was the selection of those that were to act in the capacity of the ministers, or the deacons for the ministering to the peoples, when all their material belongings had become as a part of the disciples' or Apostles' and they were all with one accord together, the entity heard much of those activities of Philip and Peter, but became closer associated with one Lucius—a kinsman of Luke. And Lucius is the entity now through whom this information is being given [Edgar Cayce].

Hence the activities and associations of the entity with Lucius became as those close activities for the founding of the ministry, the missionary activities, the influences that brought about the establishing of many portions of the Church during that early ministry of not only the disciples or Apostles but those early ministers of the Church; as Mark and Luke and Lucius and all of those—Thaddeus and Saul or Paul and Barnabas, and those of Laodicea.

For it was there that the entity went with Lucius when there was the establishings of the Church there; when Paul preached in Laodicea. For these were a portion of the kinsmen of the people from the Roman land. And there the entity ministered as the helpmeet of the wife of Lucius for those early peoples of the church there.   1468-2

In a third reading pertaining to Maraerh, Cayce relates some of the difficulties of the early church. Lucius becomes the bishop in Laodicea, appointed by Paul and Barnabus. Paul teaches celibacy for bishops. Since Mariaerh has no children, she believes many of Paul's statements are aimed at her.

Mariaerh gives birth to a son, Sylvius. The leaders later decide that Sylvius is "one chosen for service in the name of the Master." Mariaerh lives to be sixty-nine (1468-3).

According to a Cayce reading another holy woman, Marlan, often called Sardenia, arrives at the time:

> . . . when there were the preparations for the coming of the teacher, the lowly one, yet the Great *I AM* into the experience of flesh—that man might again have an advocate with the divine that had grown so far away to the hearts of those that were lost in the toils of the day.
>
> There the entity was among those peoples about the land of Bethany, during that period when Martha, Mary, and Lazarus; Bartholomew, Philip, Thomas and the others made many pilgrimages to and from the various portions of the land.
>
> The entity then was of those lands from which Bartholomew was drawn, was taken for his activities among the peoples.
>
> Hence the entity was in association with Mary, the mother; with the daughter and sons of Joseph and Mary, that made for those influences which brought the beauties into the experiences of man during that sojourn.
>
> The entity was active in the sect of the Essenes. Thus, as would be called, the entity was among the holy women— even at the days when they stood beneath the Cross, the days when they waited on those who had been persecuted, stoned and beaten for a cause.
>
> In the experience the entity was called Sardenia, but the name was Marlan.
>
> The activities of the entity made for the strength as of stone. For the entity gave much in self during the experience.   1463-2

Next, is a holy woman named Eloise, who is more of the conventional concept of such a one. Cayce says:

> The entity then was among those of the holy women and those in close acquaintanceship with many who were the teachers of the apostles or the disciples, many of those women—as Mary, Martha, Elizabeth; all of these were as friends, yea companions of the entity during the experience.
>
> For the entity then was in that capacity as one of the holy women who ministered in the temple service and in the preparation of those who dedicated their lives for individual activity during the sojourn.
>
> The entity was then what would be termed in the present, in some organizations, as a Sister Superior, or an officer as it were in those of the Essenes and their preparations.
>
> Hence we find the entity then giving, giving, ministering, encouraging, making for the greater activities; and making for those encouraging experiences oft in the lives of the Disciples; coming in contact with the Master oft in the ways between Bethany, Galilee, Jerusalem. For, as indicated, the entity kept the school on the way above Emmaus to the way that "goeth down towards Jericho" and towards the northernmost coast from Jerusalem.
>
> The name then was Eloise, and the entity blessed many of those who came to seek to know the teachings, the ways, the mysteries, the understandings; for the entity had been trained in the schools of those that were of the prophets and prophetesses, and the entity was indeed a prophetess in those experiences—thus gained throughout.
>
> Hence the stories of the experiences and activities of the Holy Women mean oft more to the entity, through the intuitive forces, through the impelling force of *good* in relationships to others . . . *Fulfill* thy purpose in thy relationship to thy maker, not to any individual, not to any group, not to any organization, not to any activity outside of self than to thy Creator!   1391-1

Again a woman is not specifically called a holy woman, but,

Veronicani's readings cause one to guess that she was one of the group. Here is her story, according to Cayce:

In that experience we find the entity was a soul seeking through those associations and activities that brought the entity into the environ of the Grecian-Syrophoenician surroundings; and in the activity in Palestine grew into womanhood there as one—that would be termed in the present—in the household of the counselor of those that traded with the peoples in that land.

With the advent of the Roman rule, the activities of such people became much more important; for there was the necessity of keeping a balance with both the Jew, the Greek and the Roman.

When the ministry of the forerunner began, that of itself brought into the association of the entity many of those that were in that particular sect of peoples to whom the entity then was joined—the Essenes.

The meeting of the mother of John and Veronicani brought about one of those friendships that made for a great deal of change in that experience, both for the entity Veronicani, and the peoples both of the Essenes and the Syrophoenicians and Grecians of that particular land.

When there were the meetings of those in the various lands where the Master taught, this caused an interest that made for much that is as the religious and commercial history of those peoples. And it is seen how that the activities of the associations brought to bear during the experience changed even the thought of the teachers in that land.

When the Master's ministry began, after the beheading of John by Herod, the entity being in the position that there were relations both in the commercial and social activities of the people made for a closer relationship that gradually grew between the sister of Lazarus and Elizabeth and the mother of the Master.

And when there were the teachings and activities in and about Bethany and in Jerusalem, there were those groups—of which the entity was a part—that gave their time in the main to making for the better associations and relations with those that particularly had been among the numbers that were healed during the ministry in that particular land. And where it is at present held as being the well of house of David in Bethany and Bethlehem, is where there was what would be termed today a place of refuge. For, as may be noted, it was one of the cities of refuge when the land was first proclaimed as the abiding place of Israel.

It then became a refuge or hospital for those that might become the teachers, the ministers, for the activities of the Essenes or teachers of which the Master was a member during the sojourn in Palestine.

With the coming of the trial and the crucifixion of the Master, when there were the periods of turmoil among those that had been the followers and teachers, and when the Roman pontiff under Cleodius disbanded or broke up the place of refuge during those periods when the trial was being brought about or being planned by the peoples, the entity then suffered the persecutions; not only because of the associations but for the heritage of the land or peoples from which the entity had been a native and a sojourner and had gained much for the native friends and associates.

When the trial arose, and when there was the preparation for the burial of the body, the entity Veronicani bathed the face of the Master. And thence arose much of that which has come as an ability in the healing and in the ministry of the soul force to those with or for whom the entity may pray or seek to aid in an hour of turmoil.

What more could be asked for, from the material, than to have bathed the face even of a dead Lord! Yet with the resurrection morning, how much greater was it to be among those to whom it was given, "Go tell my disciples that I go before them into Galilee. There shall I meet them as promised." To be among those with the mother, with the cousins, with Mary Magdala, and those that had come to anoint again the body, and find the dead Lord a risen Christ! This was the experience of the entity during that particular sojourn.

Hence oft do we find the entity and those of that particular group met in the chambers of the father of James and John, in Zebedee's rooms or hall where they met.

The entity was that one who opened the door for the doubter, Thomas, when on the third meeting with the disciples and the people in the upper chamber there was that conversation which ensued between that individual disciple and those gathered there.

During the periods when there were more and more of the persecutions that arose, the entity more and more gave of self and of those activities as related to the periods and times. And gave her son also, Stephen, that came as among the first of the martyrs for a cause. And this, while making for that period in the experience of reaching to the higher soul development, wrecked the body—and it went out into the inter-between soon after the persecutions of one Saul of Tarsus began.   489-3

Other holy women are also associated with the members of the family of Zebedee. Matada is one of these. About her, Cayce says:

The entity was among the holy women that prepared for the Master in many periods where entertainments took place in people's homes—as in the home in Cana, where there was the beginning of the miracles indicated in some interpretations of the experiences of the man Jesus in the earth, when water saw its Master, blushed and became wine even by activity! Remember, only as it was poured out would it become wine. Had it remained still, no wine would have filled those conditions where embarrassment was being brought even to the friend of the entity in that experience. For this was one of the brethren of James and John, and the entity was acquainted with the bride at that period.

With this activity there came true faith, but at times static. For there came the dependence upon the spirit without the use of the spirit by self at times. Yet the entity in the name Matada brought much help to those activities of the early church in the various centers; not only the church in Jerusalem but also in other places where there was the setting up of individual activities.   3361-1

Chapter 14

The Virgin Mary, Mother of Jesus

The visionary Emmerich presents the amazing story of Mary's Immaculate Conception beneath the Golden Gate in the subterranean passage beneath the temple. She also relates the forming of Mary's soul, which takes place almost four and one-half months after Anna's conception.

Anna is sleeping on her couch. The nun sees movement in the Holy Trinity, and as interpenetration occurs, a shining mountain rises in the figure of a human being like a beam of light before God's face. The figure shapes itself into a beautiful soul, which God shows to the angels, whose joy is beyond expression.

Next, the nun sees a beam, streaming from a light, hovering over Anna and penetrating the middle of her side. It is shaped like a human being made of light. Anna sits up immersed in light. The vision she experiences shows her body opening like a tabernacle to reveal a virgin of light from whom all salvation pours. At this precise moment, Mary moves for the first time. Anna tells Joachim what she experiences. Then she goes to pray beneath the tree where she first received the promise of a child (ACE 1 139).

The nun has other symbolical visions. After describing another picture of the Immaculate Conception, she speaks of a "stem of grace" rising above Anna with Mary and Joseph seated on the crown of the stem. Anna sits below them in a state of adoration. Above, on the summit of the tree, sits the young Jesus in shining splendor, holding the imperial globe. Emmerich sees choirs of Apostles and disciples, and, in more distant circles, other saints. Over all this are bright figures of light and unusual form, above which pour beams from a half-sun (ACE 1 145–146).

Nature always celebrates Mary's birthday around the area of Anna's house at the time of Mary's birth. A holy man first notices this annual celebration of the birds, lambs, and other creatures two hundred fifty years after Mary's death. The man meditates and prays as he travels over the Holy Land, visiting the special places involving Jesus' actions. He receives spiritual guidance and revelations. Finally, after observing the joyous chorus occurring annually between September 7 and 8, he has a vision revealing that September 8 is Mary's birth date (ACE 1 147).

Another mystery that Emmerich receives concerns a vision Adam views. In the vision, Adam witnesses a virgin appearing and restoring to Adam the forfeited salvation. This vision includes showing Moses recovering the Holy Thing and placing it in a special conveyance, which becomes the Ark of the Covenant. Like Adam, Emmerich sees this mysterious substance passing down through the ancestors of Jesus to Joachim and Anna, whom she refers to as the most holy couple of all time. Unscathed by sin at birth, Mary becomes the living Ark of the Covenant. This is a recurring image in the tapestries of the nun's visions—woven with many threads being gradually added—so as to reveal the mystery and enlighten the viewer (ACE 1 23-24).

Again, during Mary's presentation Emmerich sees the angels assisting and directing as Mary answers the questions of the priests. When the priests bless her, Mary appears transparent with a glorious halo engulfing her and containing the mystery of the Ark in a shining crystal vessel. Mary's heart appears to open like temple doors. The mysterious content of the Ark, surrounded by a temple of precious stones, seems to enter Mary's heart like the Ark entering the Holy of Holies. Then, the nun sees Mary's heart close around this sacred thing, and Mary glows with light (ACE 1 159).

Mary is four when she begins her life dedicated to spiritual guidance and practices. One of her first teachers is Naomi, a sister of the mother of Martha, Mary, and Lazarus (ACE 1 178). Mary is between twelve and thirteen when, on the stairs to the altar, she receives the designation of the angel as the one chosen to be the mother of the Messiah (5749–8).

Soon, Mary must leave the temple and prepare for marriage. Seven other virgins must also leave and marry. Mary is very sad about leaving and does not desire marriage, but she obeys. The search begins for her husband.

Isaiah 11:1 is taken quite literally: "And there shall come forth a shoot out of the stem of Jesse and a branch shall grow out of his root." Therefore, those who are candidates for being Mary's husband must hold a branch during prayers. They then place their branches on the altar. The husband will be the one whose branch blossoms. None of the branches blossom so that the search for the right husband continues. Joseph, a descendent of David, comes to the temple as requested. He receives a branch, prays, and lays the branch on the altar. As he does so a white lily–like flower blooms on the branch. Mary accepts Joseph to be her spouse (ACE 1 186–187).

The time for the wedding arrives. Joseph is thirty–six, and Mary is sixteen (5749–8). The nun, a seamstress for a number of years before taking her vows, always gives a very detailed description of the clothing people wear. She surely gives almost a photographic picture of Mary's bridal clothing and hair style. She also describes Mary as having auburn hair; finely arched dark eyebrows; a high forehead; large eyes with dark, long lashes; a delicate, straight, rather long nose; a lovely, expressive mouth; and a pointed chin, She is of medium height and moves gently but seriously (ACE 1 189).

At some point in time, the Roman Catholic Church declares Mary to be a virgin throughout her life. Certainly Joseph understands that their marriage will not be the usual type. In answer to the question as to how Joseph becomes aware of his part in the birth of Jesus, the reply is, "First by Mathias or Judah. Then as this did not coincide with his own feelings, first in a dream and then the direct voice." As to his being disturbed when Mary is with child while yet a virgin, Cayce responds:

> Owing to his natural surroundings and because of his advanced age to that of the virgin when she was given; or as would be termed in the present, because of what people say. Yet when assured, you see, that this was of the divine, not only by his brethren but by the voice and by those experiences, he knew. For you see there was from the time of the first promise, while she was still yet in training from the choice, there was a period of some three to four years; yet when he went to claim her as the bride, at the period of— or between sixteen and seventeen, she was found with child.   5749-8

Anna prepared a house for Mary and Joseph in Nazareth not far from her own house. Anna, Mary, and two of the virgins who are in the temple with Mary are in the newly arranged house. It is evening and all are praying together in a circle. Afterwards Mary ascends the steps at the back of the house to her room and prepares for prayer by dressing in a long, white, woolen garment. The nun sees her praying for a considerable amount of time and in an intense manner. With her veil lowered, she prays for the Messiah and for Redemption. Suddenly, she glances to the right to see the archangel Gabriel. The room fills with light. The nun sees Gabriel's words come from his lips as though they are formed from letters of shining light. Mary raises her veil to say, "Behold the handmaid of the Lord. May it be done unto me according to thy word!" Mary is in ecstasy. The roof vanishes and a luminous cloud appears with a pathway of light extending upward. High up, the nun perceives the Holy Trinity. At Mary's words, three streams of light come from this glorious triangle and penetrate Mary's right side then unite under her heart. Mary becomes transparent and luminous. Gabriel and the streams of light vanish, and the nun sees roses and leaves falling on Mary. Mary sees in herself (as perceived by the nun) the tiny glowing human form, complete to the perfect little fingers. It is midnight. The women enter the room but, seeing Mary in ecstasy, they withdraw. Mary goes to the wall altar, lowers the swathed child image, and prays. She lies down much later. Anna perceives what is occurring. Mary receives much knowledge by intuition and understands much of what is happening and what will happen. She knows that the Redeemer conceived within her will have to one day suffer and die. Meanwhile the nun receives the explanation as to why Jesus has to be nine months in the womb, go through childhood, and not be born a perfect man like Adam. The Fall causes conception and birth to be so unholy that the Son of God must cleanse the whole process to make it Holy once again. It is necessary for a woman to be conceived without sin before the Redeemer can come, and Mary is the first woman to be so conceived and born. The nun thinks about the change of events that make it taboo for a woman to set foot in the temple of Jerusalem. But in Nazareth a virgin is the temple and within her rests the Most Holy (ACE 1 104–196).

Joseph and Mary are in the house Anna provides for them. Joseph has his apartment in the front of the house, and Mary has hers in the back separated from the other part by a fireplace. After the wedding, Joseph goes to Bethlehem on business. When he returns, Anna has a feast for them and several guests (ACE 1 190).

Mary has a strong desire to see Elizabeth, her cousin, and she and Joseph start on a journey to Hebron. Elizabeth does not know Mary except through hearsay. Elizabeth learns in a vision that a woman is to give birth to the Messiah. She begins to think of Mary and have a strong desire to see her. She is much older than Mary and is pregnant with John. Zachary returns home. Joseph and Mary arrive. The two men converse; Zachary uses the tablet since he cannot speak. They persuade Joseph to stay eight days before returning home. When Elizabeth and Mary embrace, the nun sees light streaming between them. Elizabeth steps back and exclaims to Mary, "Blessed art thou among women, and blessed is the fruit of thy womb." In response, Mary recites a canticle of thanksgiving. Elizabeth tells Mary that the infant in her womb leaps for joy at the sound of Mary's voice. The two women have many spiritual experiences together. Joseph returns home, and Mary stays three months until John is born but returns to Nazareth soon after the birth.

Joseph receives directions in a vision that he is to take Mary to Bethlehem where the baby will be born. He tells Mary and Anna about the commands. Anna is upset, but Mary feels all along that she must give birth in Bethlehem. She studies all the prophecies concerning the Messiah's birth with the holy women teaching her in the temple. She understands that since sin enters the world because of a woman's actions, that now the atonement is to come by way of a woman. Soon, the couple starts on their journey with Mary riding on a donkey and as per instructions, a year-old donkey freely moves ahead of them leading the way. The weather is cold, and Mary prays they will not freeze. She is immediately filled with warmth and stretches out her hands to warm Joseph (ACE 1 209–211).

In the crib cave, Mary sends Joseph to pray. The nun reports on many visions various people are seeing in different places. Anna is the only one who knows the baby is being born in Bethlehem. Mary kneels to pray and give birth. Light envelopes Mary, who rises above the ground. Jesus is born. He is a shining little infant, lying on the rug at Mary's knees and seems to be growing within dazzling light. Mary soon spreads a cover over the baby. After a while the baby moves and cries. Angels encircle Mary as she lifts the baby and cover and envelopes the two of them in her veil while she suckles Him. It is possibly an hour before Mary calls to Joseph, still prostrate in prayer (ACE 1 227).

In time, Joseph takes Mary and Jesus to the temple for the purification ceremony. They take an offering of fruit and doves in a partitioned basket. The ceremony is quite elaborate and involves Anna, Naomi (Mary's teacher), old Simeon the priest, and others. Simeon has a vision the night before the holy family arrives, in which an angel tells him to pay particular attention to the first child presented the next morning. That child, he learns, is the long–awaited Messiah, and after seeing Him, Simeon will soon die. This does occur, and Simeon's three sons eventually become Jesus' disciples (ACE 1 281–283).

Besides the earthly purification ceremony, the nun also sees in a vision the purification ceremony in the spiritual church. Angelic choirs fill the church with the Holy Trinity above them in the center. Below, in the center, there is an altar on which is a tree with wide leaves. These remind the nun of the tree in Eden which contributes to Adam's fall. The Virgin, holding Jesus, floats up to the altar. The tree bows low before her and begins to wither. A glorious angel comes to Mary. She gives Jesus to the angel to place on the altar. The Holy Trinity glows. Mary receives from the angel, a shining globe with an image of a swathed child on it. The angel hovers over the altar, holding the gift, and from all sides, poor people come bearing lights. The lights seem to pass into the child on the ball and then reappear. The lights join to become one and extend over Mary and Jesus and light everything so as to cover the whole earth. The nun believes that the Tree of Knowledge withering when Mary appears, and the Holy Trinity being offered Jesus signify the reuniting of humanity with God. Because of Mary, the many lights become one in Jesus who illumines all (ACE 1 286).

It is not necessary to repeat the many parts of Mary's story already told. Of course, as the holiest of all holy women ever, she deserves full attention, but with her great modesty and her complete obedience to and interior communication with God, she would be the first to turn from being a central focus. Although the nun fully acknowledges that Mary Heli is an older sister of Mary, she does not have any visions regarding the children born to Mary and Joseph. We must look to the Cayce readings (and to a small extent, the Bible) to learn of Jesus' half-siblings.

In Mark 6:3 these questions are asked of Jesus, as He teaches in the synagogue: "Is he not the carpenter, the son of Mary, and the brother of James and Joses and Judas and Simon: and behold, are not his sisters here with us? And they denounced him." Jesus answered, "There is no prophet who is belittled, except in his own city and among his own brothers and in his own house." The passage in Matthew 13:55–57 is very similar: "Is he not the carpenter's son? Is not his mother called Mary? and his brothers, James and Joses and Simon and Judah? Are not all his sisters with us? Where did he get all these things? And they were perplexed about him. But Jesus said to them, No prophet is mocked except in his own city and in his own house." Matthew 12:46 implies that Jesus has brothers: "While he was speaking to the people his mother and his brothers came and stood outside, and wanted to speak with him." To this Jesus gives the well known reply in verse 50: "For whosoever does the will of my Father in heaven is my brother and my sister and my mother."

When the nun is telling of Anna visiting Mary, Joseph, and Jesus in the crib cave, she makes a curious comment that is not repeated. She claims that Anna bears a son by her third husband and that he becomes known as the brother of Christ. She does not name the son nor give any other information about him. Perhaps Joses is this person and explains the extra son of Mary named in the Bible but not in the Cayce readings. By calling Joses the son of Anna, the nun is not disputing the Roman Catholic Church claim that Mary is a virgin for life (ACE 1 276).

These questions are answered during a reading Edgar Cayce gives:

> (Q) At what time after this birth of Jesus did Mary and Joseph take up the normal life of a married couple, and bring forth the issue called James?
> (A) Ten years. Then they came in succession; James, the daughter, Jude . . .
> (Q) Was Mary *required* to wait ten years before knowing Joseph?
> (A) Only, you see, until Jesus went to be taught by others did the normal or natural associations come; not required— it was a choice of them both because of their *own* feelings.
> But when He was from without the roof and under the protection of those who were the guides (that is, the priests), these associations began then as normal experiences.
>
> 5749-8

These same three children are also mentioned in reading 5749-7. The Bible names four sons with one called Judas in Mark and probably the same son called Judah in Matthew. Jude is no doubt another name for the same son, and only three sons are named.. In none of these instances is a girl named, and only one is implied (the daughter) in the Cayce readings, while more than one is implied in the quotes from the Bible. Obviously, giving identity to women and assigning importance to women carries little weight in biblical times—as we see from this study where so few of the holy women receive mention in the Bible.

The person known as Jude receives about one hundred twenty-six readings from Edgar Cayce. At least seven of those readings include information about Jude. "Just before this, we find this entity in the days when the Master came into the Promised Land. This entity one that followed close in the ways of the teachings as set by Him. In the personage of the brother in the flesh, Jude." (137-4) In another reading Cayce relates:

> There have been times and occasions when there was the physical resistance against the accepting of the tenets as presented; yet in this later view there is seen that which brings to the subconscious forces that awakening of the experiences of the entity, in the death of that One that presented the way to the giving of self to the service of man, in the Son of man, and the brother of entity; and in the flesh there comes, in the year and a half after this death, the acknowledgement of the Master as the Master of the entity, and in that day the entity then only nineteen, as is viewed by the entity. As is seen by reading that as was composed by the entity in that period, and set down now in the sacred Scriptures [Jude 1-25], there is seen that the entity in that period was the deep thinker, and one that sought out many conditions as had been presented through the knowledge of ancient days . . .
> (Q) Did I live on earth at the time of Christ's crucifixion?
> (A) As the brother.   137-64

More information about Jude appears in Ruth's readings. Information regarding James appears in readings for others, but that entity who is the brother of Jesus does not have his own reading. A young man receives a reading and is told that during the time of Jesus, "The entity then of the household of the brother of the Lord, in that of James the Less, in the name Clement." (1715-3) Whether Clement is a son of James is not clear. In another reading during the time that the disciples are widely dispersed, the entity—a woman named Patience—was:

> Among those of the Arab land, and to whose household
> Andrew and James came during those first periods of the
> activities. This was James the Less, not the brother of John
> but the brother of the Lord, that came in those activities—
> and the entity learned much of those from those experi-
> ences.   1431-1

A reading for Susane, a holy woman of Capernaum, tells us she is acquainted with the household of Joseph and Mary. She is about the age of Ruth and a close friend. Also she knows Jude and James (1179-8).

In a reading for Mariaerh, wife of Lucius, there is a reference to James, the brother of the Lord, being head of the church in Jerusalem. Lucius' sister, Nimmuo, also knows James.

> With the establishing of the church at Jerusalem, the entity
> was present when James—the brother of the Lord—was
> raised to that position or place as the head of the church
> through the direct affluence of James and John, the sons
> of Zebedee. *This* brought about that first of the authorities
> putting forth their hand and slaying James by the sword.
> This happened not by that of trial, but by that as would be
> called a riot, and not incorrectly were James and John
> called the sons of thunder.   2390-3

According to Cayce, Nimmuo spent most of her tine ". . . either in the direct companionship of the brother or of the holy women and their associates, their friends, in and around Jerusalem." (2390-3)

Cayce gives to the woman named as Jesus' sister Ruth at least ten readings. In one of these readings, he says:

> Before that, then, we find comes the experience that is the
> outstanding one—of a glory, yet of a suffering, turmoils,
> yet joy; beautiful experiences, yet sorrow and shame.
>   For the entity was in that land where the Master walked,

and the daughter of Mary the mother of the Lord—Ruth . . .

In the experience as the entity became the more closely associated with those in authority from the civil forces, or the Roman influences through those experiences after the death upon the cross, and after the periods of those beautiful experiences with the disciples and the apostles, there came then that helpful aid in the entity's activity as it journeyed with those that would aid and bring to account much of those forces that brought to the powers of the Roman period the awareness of the Christ influence as exemplified in the *man* Jesus . . .

Yet the forces as in the experience of Ruth, that colaborer with the mother of the Master, are the outstanding ones . . .

(Q) Did I know the Roman who walked with Christ to Emmaus?

(A) Married the one. With him then the entity returned to Rome, as has been indicated, aiding in the interpreting, in helping others to understand the message that Jesus brought.   1158-2

Another reading for Ruth reveals not only more about her but her whole family.

The reading refers to the return of Joseph and Mary, the father and mother of Ruth.

For soon after the return, and that recorded in Writ of the journey to the city for that period of the Passover teachings, we find that James—the elder brother of the entity—was born into that experience.

In the next year, when there had been by the Wise Men of the East the beginnings of the teachings of Jesus and his sojourn in Persia, India, and when those activities brought about the change in the material or financial status of the family, Ruth then was born—in that city of Capernaum; and surrounded with the activities that befitted the peoples of that period, that day.

There was awe in the minds of the peoples as to what had taken place at the birth of the mother's, or Mary's, first son.

Hence the entity, Ruth, was rather in awe of the suggestions, the intimations that surrounded that experience; and questioned the mother concerning same.

As the entity grew into maidenhood, and after the birth of Jude, then the death of Joseph brought that brother—Jesus—home! And there were those activities that surrounded the entity concerning that unknown, that strange kinsman; that kinsman whom the peoples held in awe, yet said many unkind things about him.

With the departure of that brother to Egypt for the final initiations of teachings, with John—another kinsman who had been spoken of and held in awe, his mother having been a chosen vessel by the priests of the Essenes, and he, John, being the lineal descendent of the high priests of the Jews—we find that in the entity's latter teen ages such ponderings brought a great many disturbing influences to the entity, Ruth . . .

Hence we find the entity was divided in thought and activity between those tenets held by the elder brother, James, those held by the mother, and the actual activities of the entity as one among those of a peoples that were being questioned and doubted!

With the return of John, the cousin, and the beginning of his ministry—one that had renounced his position as a priest that might serve in the temple, to become an outcast and a teacher in the wilderness—to the entity Ruth, there was brought consternation.

And again there was a questioning with the mother as to those experiences of the mother preceding the birth of that Jesus.   1158-4

This long reading of Ruth continues to explain that when Jesus returns to Capernaum after the wilderness test and the meeting with John, Ruth hears Jesus teach in the synagogue about the prophecies of Isaiah, Jeremiah, and others. He applies them to the experiences of the times in which they are living.

Jesus' teachings raise quite a stir among the people, including Ruth. Very soon, she meets a Roman involved in the supervision of determining who qualifies to pay tribute to Rome. He is handsome and unusual in his sympathy for the unfortunate. Ruth wants her mother to learn of this man's philosophy and his knowledge of a world quite different from theirs. Ruth somewhat resents her mother's counsel and feels her friend has greater knowledge than either the Essenes or the orthodox Jewish people. Ruth attempts to check out the truth of the happenings in Bethlehem and in Bethany.

Then comes the raising of Lazarus, which Ruth and her Roman friend experience. This creates a whole new understanding of the relationship between God and man. About this, Cayce says:

> *Then*, just before the crucifixion, there was the consummation of the wedding between Ruth and that friend, now the husband—then the husband [1151].
>
> And *Jesus* attended *that* wedding also; blessed them.
>
> And with the recall of the companion to Rome, during those experiences in Rome, the crucifixion came about.
>
> With the return and the recall of Pilate before the authorities in Rome, with the meeting again of Ruth with the mother and the holy women—and Lazarus, Mary, and Martha, the friends of the mother—and those periods with Elizabeth, the mother of John the kinsman—there were the greater effects from the emotional as well as the active forces brought into the experience of the entity, Ruth.
>
> 1158-4

This reading continues, and other readings give more information for this sister of Jesus and Philoas, her Roman husband. Both walked with Jesus to Emmaus.

Ruth certainly knows many of the holy women but is not specifically named as one of them. Apparently, she and Philoas do much to help people and stand by the early Christians as the persecutions increase.

The woman who received these readings about Ruth appeared at the

A.R.E. when she was one hundred years old and spoke to the conferees, even reciting poetry from memory. Surely, as Ruth she earned the title, holy woman.

The final illness of Joseph brings Jesus back to the family. He is around thirty years of age. The nun frequently sees Mary and Jesus with Joseph, tending to his needs and giving him a little food and something to drink from a mug. As Joseph starts breathing his last, Mary sits at the head of the bed holding Joseph in her arms. Jesus stands near Joseph's side. The room fills with light and angels. At death Joseph's hands are crossed on his chest. A winding sheet covers him completely, and he is laid in a narrow casket. Some good man donates a beautiful tomb, and Jesus and Mary and a few men follow the coffin to the tomb. Many angels accompany the body. Later the Christians remove the body and bury Joseph at Bethlehem.

The nun believes Joseph could not endure Jesus' crucifixion as he is so loving and gentle and suffers whenever he sees the Jews filled with jealousy and unable to stand the sight of Jesus. Mary also suffers much from all these slights and persecutions. But Jesus' love is unconditional and He pursues His mission in spite of all.

Since the Pharisees in Nazareth side against Jesus and call Him a vagrant, Jesus and Mary move to a small village between Capernaum and Bethsaida and live in a house given to Jesus by Levi. Family members, including Mary Cleophas and her sons, Simon, James, Thaddeus, and Joses Barsabas all came to comfort Mary and Jesus on the death of Joseph. The sons all follow John the Baptist (ACE 1 330–332).

Although we know very little about the children of Mary and Joseph, we learn a great deal about Jesus and His mother Mary. He treats her with great respect, which she certainly deserves. She suffers greatly when He is mistreated, which is quite often.

Maraha, Anna's youngest sister, and her family live in Sephoris in the former house of her parents four hours from Nazareth. Jesus and three disciples stop at His great aunt's house. Mary, Mary Cleophas, and some other women are already there. The city has sects of Pharisees, Sadducees, and Essenes. Jesus stays and preaches several days and urges people to go to John for baptism. In the Pharisee synagogue, there is a separate place for women. The Pharisees murmur against Jesus' words. Jesus is received kindly by the Essenes in their synagogue; there is no separate place for women. Next, Jesus goes to the Sadducees who have a school near the synagogue where the city's large number of lunatics, possessed, and demoniacs attend. They have to attend teaching at the synagogue in a rear hall. Guards with whips keep this pitiful audience orderly. Jesus appears and all are quiet. Then, these outcasts start speaking out regarding Jesus' life. The whips of the guards will not stop them. Jesus commands them to be brought to Him outside the synagogue and to bring all the rest of these unfortunate souls forming a big audience. Jesus announces that the spirit calling out through these people comes from the lower regions, and He orders that spirit to return below. Immediately all are cured and some fall to the ground.

Great excitement fills the city. Is it because of gratitude and amazement that Jesus can instantly facilitate the cure of all these deranged people? This is not the case. Jesus and His followers are in immediate danger. Jesus manages to escape and hide in a house, then leaves the city after dark. His mother and the disciples, Maraha's two sons, Cocharia and Aristaria, also leave the city. Mary is greatly troubled as she sees Jesus receive His most violent persecution yet. They all meet at a certain grove of trees and go on to Bethany (ACE 1 350–352).

Some of the most surprising information in the visions of the nun concerns the fact that Mary travels about the country in considerable support of Jesus' ministry with the other holy women. All seem to like gathering at the home of Lazarus and Martha. It is at this house that Jesus has a private conversation with His mother. He informs her He is starting his mission by going to John's baptism. He will return for a brief time in the area of Samaria and then go to the desert for forty days. This makes Mary quite uneasy, and she begs Him not to go as He might die of hunger and thirst. He tells her in a very loving manner that she must not seek to concern herself about His human considerations. He is now to commence His mission in a very concerted manner, and those who adhere to Him will suffer greatly. Although He will love her always, He is now focusing on the plan set by His Heavenly Father. No doubt a sword will pierce her soul, but she, too, must adhere to the commands of God. Although greatly troubled, Mary as always, resigns herself to God's will and Jesus' bidding (ACE 1 405–406).

While Jesus dwells in the desert, Mary resides near Capernaum and is subjected to all the gossip about Him: He is a wanderer; He neglects His mother; His disciples are scattered. But Mary always maintains an internal vision of Jesus, contemplating His actions and sharing His suffering (ACE 2 19). One of the reasons Mary urges Jesus to attend the wedding at Cana and be with many of His friends and relatives is to end this criticism of Jesus. Jesus does attend, supplies some of the food, and invites such friends as Lazarus and Martha to attend. Actually, Lazarus pays for the feast expenses Jesus incurs. The wedding festivities last three days and give an opportunity for Jesus' followers and relatives to become acquainted. He is very much involved in the affair and plays the part of Master of the feast. He advises the guests on the responsibilities of marriage, of continence, chastity, and spiritual unions. The time comes when Mary learns the wine is depleted, and she calls on Jesus to replenish it. There is much symbolism involved in the miracle of the wine Jesus provides at the request of Mary that has to do with the future church. The entire wedding is filled with symbolism related to the events to be fulfilled in the lives of Jesus and the people present (ACE 2 48–59).

Mary's life as a widow involves sewing, knitting, spinning, praying, giving consolation to those in distress, instructing women, and living on the gifts of her friends as she no longer owns fields or cattle. She travels fairly frequently with other holy women. A group of women accompany Jesus and several disciples to a small city called Dothain. After an entertainment and a meal, the women leave for Capernaum. Jesus privately takes leave of His mother. The nun reports that when they are alone, Jesus embraces His mother on arrival or departure, but if others attend, then He just clasps her hand or nods His head in acknowledgment. The nun describes Mary at that time as still being youthful looking, delicately built, and rather tall. Her forehead is quite high and her nose long. She has large eyes, beautiful red lips, a rather dark but beautiful complexion with rose tinged cheeks (ACE 2 93, 95–97).

Another time the nun makes some comparisons of the beauty of some of the women. She states that Magdalen is a taller more beautiful woman than the others. Dina the Samaritan seems to have a better disposition as she is more dexterous and active, eager to help, cheerful, affectionate, and humble. But the Blessed Virgin is marvelously beautiful, not just externally but because she is modest, sweet, gentle, earnest, and unpretentious. Because of her purity, she reflects the image of God. She appears innocent, grave, wise, devout, and noble. Certainly as Emmerich sees Mary in her great number of visions, she is an outstanding model of womanhood (ACE 2 493–484). Additionally, the nun comments on Mary's admirable simplicity and states that Jesus does not distinguish her in the presence of others but does always treat her with reverence. Mary rarely seeks people out socially but focuses on the sick or ignorant to be of help to them. She always conducts herself with humility, simplicity, and thoughtfulness. She is quiet and meditative. Even the enemies respect her (ACE 3 73).

The concept of eating the flesh and drinking the blood of Jesus giving everlasting life causes great confusion and dissension among the Pharisees. They reject that God sent Him. Jesus explains many statements of the prophets and connects the accomplishments of John the Baptist with the prophecies. People ask more questions of Jesus—many regarding when He will feed them His body and blood. Even the disciples cannot fully understand and say to Jesus that the concept is hard to comprehend. He replies that they will witness more wonderful things but that many of the faithful will abandon Him to His enemies. However, He will not abandon His unfaithful disciples.

Mary and other women attend these discourses. Mary, by interior consciousness, comprehends these mysteries. After all she gives birth to the Second Person of the Godhead, and she carries all this knowledge in her heart with humility and reverence. She prays for those who listen to Jesus without comprehension. The nun then sees the disciples separate from Jesus. Two Kingdoms appear: the one of Christ and the one of Satan. The latter is magnificent with its harlots, prophets, kings, emperors and priests—with Satan on a lavish throne. The nun sees Christ's kingdom on earth as poor and unimpressive with much misery and suffering. She sees Mary as the Church and Christ on the Cross. He is like a church—the wound in His side like the entrance (ACE 3 230-231). Emmerich feels the Scriptures give only an outline of the important doctrines, which Jesus spends hours explaining to His followers (ACE 3 289). In one of these sessions, Jesus explains quite extensively to His Apostles and disciples that He is conceived by the Holy Ghost. He continues to speak reverently of His pure, holy Mother. He exclaims that they live in a happy and holy time because the relationship between God and man is again established. To claim that bond, each must accept the Christ and reject worldly temptations. Only with that partnership can Satan's power be overwhelmed (ACE 3 309).

Jesus returns to Capernaum along with about thirty disciples. Many Jews from Cyprus arrive. Jewish emigrants arrive from Ornithopolis. Three young pagan philosophers come with James the Less and Thaddeus. Jesus usually presents new converts to His mother. She and Jesus understand intuitively that she must take a very active role as spiritual mother to these disciples, taking them into her heart, her prayers, and her blessings, much as though they are brothers of Jesus and thus her own offspring. Mary does this wholeheartedly, and Jesus solemnly treats her as a holy, adoptive, spiritual mother expanding her family (ACE 3 444-445).

After much teaching in synagogues and instructing of Apostles and disciples, Jesus and the disciples go toward Bethsaida and stop at an inn where the Blessed Virgin, the widow of Nain, and other women are waiting to see Him before he goes to teach on the other side of the Jordan. Mary speaks privately with Jesus, and weeping, begs Him not to go to Jerusalem for the temple dedication feast. She fears for His safety, but He embraces her and gently and lovingly consoles her. He reminds her that she is His mother so that He can come and fulfill His Father's assigned mission. He urges her to continue to be strong and courageous as an example to the others. He then blesses the other women, and they leave for Capernaum (ACE 3 461).

Jesus and His disciples are traveling and teaching. At a little mountain village toward Juttah, Jesus goes straight to the synagogue to teach. The priests try to prevent it, but the people want to hear Him on the subject of no man being able to serve two masters. He states that He has come to bring a sword upon earth in order to separate out all that is bad. The disciples listen and learn along with the people (ACE 3 481). Shortly after this gathering in a place near Samaria, His mother and Mary Cleophas come to spend the Sabbath with Jesus, and they learn of the death of Lazarus.

Emmerich makes a comment on Mary's habits while in prayer. She says that up to the time of the conception of the Savior, when the Blessed Virgin prays, she stands with her hands crossed over her breast, and with her eyes lowered. Then, after the holy Incarnation, she usually kneels with her face turned toward heaven and her hands uplifted (ACE 3 500).

Many times Jesus teaches on marriage. Modern couples will not likely agree with His instruction, but He presents much food for thought to a presently very troubled institution. Perhaps, some of His statements reflect on Eve, whose disobedience causes a rupture in the relationship between God and the couple He has created. Eve's disobedience causes terrible pain to subsequent generations. Discord in marriage and failure to produce good, pure offspring is principally the wife's fault. It is her lot to suffer, endure, and to form and preserve the fruit of marriage. She must labor spiritually to gain victory over self in order to perfect her soul and the fruit of her womb. Thus, she can eliminate any evil in her soul, which is essential, since on her whole conduct depends the blessing or destruction of her children. Marriage is not for sensual gratification but for penance and mortification. It requires constant fear about the encroachment of sin and constant warfare through prayer and self-conquest. As the mother obtains victories over self, her children will be victorious over self as well (ACE 3 505).

Also in this area of Sichar-Cedar, the nun believes that the people's ancestors must be aware of the Ark of the Covenant since they ask Jesus to tell them the whereabouts of the Holy Mystery abiding in the Ark. His very interesting answer is that because so much of it passed into mankind, it can no longer be found. The conclusion to be reached from this is that the Messiah is born. Many of the people in this area believe the Messiah died among the Innocents destroyed by Herod (ACE 3 513).

Jesus never baptized anyone. Repentance is the purpose of John's baptising. Women for the most part receive baptism only after Pentecost. Mary, Jesus' mother, receives it alone by John at the Pool of Bethsaida after Pentecost. Before the baptism, John celebrates Holy Mass by consecrating and reciting some prayers (ACE 3 583).

Several disciples leave Bethany to go meet Jesus in Bethabara. Mary approaches Judas as he prepares to leave. She talks with him earnestly about being more moderate, to be mindful of his thoughts and actions and to resist interfering as he so often does. Later, she offers prayer for him after he betrays her Son (ACE 3 595).

Jesus returns to Bethany and goes to the temple to teach. His mother walks part way with Him. He begins to prepare her for His coming Passion. He tells her that Simeon's prophecy of a sword piercing her soul is about to occur. She will see all befall Him including the maltreatment and torturous death. Mary is, of course, very grievously troubled (ACE 4 1). In His last times with His disciples Jesus predicts many things that will happen very soon. He says His mother will suffer with Him and names specifics. He tells Peter that he will also suffer much, but he will stand as head of the Community or Church, which will greatly increase. Peter, James the Less, and John will remain for three years with the faithful in Jerusalem. Persecutions will arise against Lazarus and the holy women. Thomas and Matthew will go to Ephesus to prepare for the day when Jesus' mother and many of His followers will go there to live. The thought of Mary living in Ephesus seems quite strange to them. Jesus asks Nathanael to write down the predictions he is presenting to them.

The day before the entry into Jerusalem, Jesus, Peter, John, James, Lazarus, Mother Mary, and six holy women conceal themselves in the subterranean apartments at Lazarus's house. They do this because of a prohibition against anyone harboring Jesus and His followers issued by Caiaphas and his cohorts (ACE 4 11).

The procession proceeds toward Jerusalem. The holy women are at the rear with Mary leading them (ACE 4 16).

Jesus tells the Apostles that after this last Pasch or Passover for him, He is going to His Father. Peter asks if His mother will be going with

Him. They all revere and love Mary very much. Jesus replies that she will remain some years longer. The nun believes He indicates fifteen years more (ACE 4 39).

After going to the temple in Jerusalem for the last time and weeping with the Apostles, Jesus and the followers return to Bethany. The women serve the meal, not keeping themselves separate as previously. The next day about sixty disciples gather. The middle of the afternoon, Jesus and the Apostles serve the meal to the others. Mary and her niece are full of grief because that very morning Jesus confides to Mary that His death will soon occur. They leave for the disciples' inn. At the meal, Jesus announces His approaching death and predicts what will follow that event. All are very sorrowful and weeping. He speaks of His mother, whose great compassion will cause her to suffer with Him all the torture of His bitter death, but she will have to live on for years (ACE 4 42).

Jesus sends Peter and John to Jerusalem to prepare for the Paschal feast. He then takes a solemn leave of the holy women and Lazarus in Bethany, giving them final instructions and admonitions. He speaks alone with Mary, who begs Him to be merciful when He speaks of Judas' treachery. She also implores Him to let her die with Him. He tells He will rise again and just where He will then appear to her. He embraces her and thanks her for her deep love (ACE 4 55-56).

It is time for the last supper, which the nun describes in great detail. Jesus consecrates Peter and John and tells them they will later consecrate the other Apostles. This is a secret gathering with Jesus teaching many concepts and ceremonial practices. The holy women sit in a separate room. The Chalice kept by Veronica is put to use. Jesus institutes the Blessed Sacrament, explaining that the sacrifice of Moses and the significance of the Paschal lamb will be fulfilled, and they will come out of bondage. Many secret and mysterious actions and explanations surround all the ceremony. Although Mary sits in a nearby room, the nun sees Jesus present the bread and wine to her, and then she vanishes from the room. She is not baptized until after the Resurrection (ACE 4 58-78).

Although Mary, Mary Cleophas, and Magdalen plead with Jesus not to go to the Mount of Olives for fear of arrest, Jesus and the Apostles head there, and the women go to the house of Mary Marcus (ACE 4 80–88).

As Jesus prays in great anguish at Mt. Olivet in a grotto, He sees the past, present, and future sins of those He will redeem by His crucifixion. He sees their ingratitude and their abandonment of His bride, the Church, and the corruption of Christendom (ACE 4 80).

As He prays and sweats blood in the grotto, Jesus sees and feels His Blessed Mother in great anguish and sorrow as she suffers with Him by interior participation and uninterrupted union. An angel comes to Him with a chalice above which is a shining morsel. The angel places the morsel in Jesus' mouth and has Him drink from the chalice, and then the angel disappears. This is the symbolic acceptance of His Passion, and He is strengthened (ACE 4 108).

While the holy women are on the streets in the night seeking word of Jesus, Pilate listens to reports and issues orders. Meanwhile, his wife, Claudia Procla sleeps and produces troubled dreams (ACE 4 136).

John finds Mary at Martha's house and tells her Caiaphas has condemned Jesus to death. Mary wants to go where she can see her Son. John takes her and some of the holy women to Caiaphas's judgment hall. On the way they have to pass the workmen, cursing because they have to work by torchlight to construct Jesus' cross. As painful as the sight is to Mary, she prays for those wretches. At the outer court, a closed door stands between them and where Jesus is being held before being taken to the prison below. At last the door opens, and Peter comes out with the crowd. He has just denied Jesus three times, and here is Mary asking about Jesus. At last, he cries out that Jesus is condemned to death, and he, Peter, has denied him thrice (ACE 4 164–166).

Mary and companions hurry ahead by a different way to be where Jesus will pass on His way to Pilate. The procession reaches them, and Mary is totally shocked by the sight of her maltreated, bloody Son. She cries out, "Is this my Son?" He casts an emotional glance toward her (ACE 4 180). They all hurry on toward Pilate's judgment seat, still early in the morning. The story is well known that Pilate has contempt for the Jews and their treatment of Jesus. When he learns Jesus is from Galilee, he immediately orders Jesus to be taken to Herod, whose territory includes Galilee. Herod is in Jerusalem for the feast. At this time, Claudia Procla, Pilate's wife is trying to speak with him.

The two meet in the summer house behind the palace. The wife of Pilate pleads with him to do nothing to injure Jesus. She tells Pilate at length of her visions during the night—visions that include the Annunciation to Mary, the murder of the Innocents, Jesus' time in the desert, and many other scenes that involve the sanctity and anguish of Mary. Then, when she sees the mob the next morning, she recognizes Jesus as the one in her visions. The astonished Pilate compares her vision with his observations. He declares that he will not condemn Jesus because he sees Him as an innocent victim of wicked Jews. Then he gives his wife some item as a pledge of that promise. They part. Pilate rushes to his pagan gods and begins to vacillate (ACE 4 194–196).

Meanwhile, Mary begs John and Magdalen to walk with her upon the path where Jesus suffers after His arrest. They cover the entire route from Caiaphas' judgment hall on to Annas's palace, then through Ophel to Gethsemane on Mount Olivet. Wherever Jesus falls, His mother kisses the earth. Magdalen and John watch tearfully and assist Mary as best they can. This is the origin of the Holy Way of the Cross as first walked by His mother, who agrees to bear a Son to be sacrificed in such a cruel manner for the Redemption of mankind. The nun claims that Mary is the concurrent cause of our salvation, our Redemptrix (ACE 4 191–192).

Herod allows Jesus to be further abused after Jesus will not answer his questions. The nun states that she receives the revelation that Jesus refuses to answer Herod because of his adulterous relationship with his brother's wife Herodias, and because of the murder of John the Baptist. Both Annas and Caiaphas use Jesus' silence to renew the charges against Him. Herod has no use for these two, feels remorse for John's murder, and secretly fears Jesus. Politically, he does not want to condemn Jesus to death because of Pilate declaring Him guiltless. He sends Jesus back to Pilate. Immediately, the High Priests put considerable money in the hands of Jesus' enemies and send them to bribe the Pharisees (many from other cities for the Passover) to go to Pilate's palace and clamor for Jesus' death. The soldiers also receive money to abuse Jesus. The nun sees weeping angels ministering to Jesus, keeping Him alive (ACE 4 199–202).

Once more Jesus stands before Pilate. Claudia Procla sends a servant to remind Pilate of his promise not to condemn Jesus. John, Mary, and the holy women stand weeping in a corner of the hall. Mary knows Jesus must complete His mission but still suffers as does Jesus. Pilate plans to have Jesus chastised and let Him go. The nun describes the beating and scourging Jesus receives in painful detail. At one point, a relative of a blind man cured by Jesus rushes forward and cries to the drunken executioners not to beat this innocent man to death. While the startled torturers pause, he quickly cuts Jesus lose from the pillar so that He falls unconscious in a pool of His own blood. All this horror Mary suffers with Jesus but in a state of ecstasy. Her sister, Mary Heli, holds her in her arms while Mary Cleophas leans on her mother's arm. The holy women, overcome with grief, gather around the Blessed Mother and her relatives. At this point. Claudia Procla sends a large bundle of linen cloths to Mary, perhaps hoping Jesus will be released, and the women can bind up His torn flesh. The executioners drive Jesus past the women. He manages to wipe the blood from His eyes to see His mother. She reaches out toward Him as the torturers drag Him away. Magdalen and Mary, surrounded by the other women, take the linens given by Pilate's wife and soak up the sacred blood of Jesus. There are about twenty holy women, and it is about nine in the morning when the scourging ends (ACE 4 208–215).

The nun sees Claudia Procla send Pilate's pledge to him and declare herself free from her husband. That same evening she secretly leaves the palace and goes to the holy women, who conceal her in the subterranean area of Lazarus' house. Later, she becomes a special friend of Paul and follows him (ACE 4 240).

While the nun is having these visions of the Passion from February 18, 1823, to March 8, 1823, she remains in continual ecstasy, suffering along with Jesus. She lies unconscious of external affairs, sobbing copiously while perspiring so profusely as to saturate her clothes and bedding. Her thirst is great so that she can barely speak and tells her visions in fragments (ACE 4 215).

During the horrible period of suffering, the nun sees the Blessed Virgin with pale, haggard cheeks and eyes bloodshot from weeping. In spite of her frantic travels over Jerusalem, her dress is neat and proper. She looks dignified and noble. Her beauty is of a superhuman combination of purity, truth, and holiness (ACE 4 224–228).

The nun's more terrible, detailed description continues of Jesus' treatment when He again appears before Pilate. Due to the demands of the bribed and misled crowd, Pilate washes his hands, condemns Jesus to death, and releases Barabas. Mary, John, and the holy women hear and observe in utter despair. They leave the scene, and Mary again requests going over the path taken by the tortured Jesus. Her tears at each spot where Jesus falls consecrate the places (ACE 4 228–239).

Jesus arrives where the cross lies on the ground. He falls on His knees, embraces and kisses the cross and gives a prayer of thanksgiving to His Heavenly Father that the Redemption of mankind is underway. The procession leading Jesus goes through narrow back streets so as not to interfere with the people going to the temple for the slaughtering of the Paschal lamb (ACE 4 244).

Again, Mary begs John to take her where she can see Jesus pass by. Some of the executioner's servants carrying the tools of the crucifixion, upon learning Mary's identity, thrust the long nails at her and jeer at her. When Jesus appears, His mother rushes to Him, falls on her knees and throws her arms around Him. "My Son!"—"My Mother!" Some of the soldiers are touched, and while ordering her away they make no move to lay hands on her. John and the women lead her away (ACE 4 251).

Mary and about seventeen of the holy women, following the way of the cross, stop at Veronica's house to view the imprinted veil. At last they arrive at the site of the crucifixion and see the cross, the hammers, the ropes, the nails, and no end of drunken executioners. The crosses of the two thieves lie ready, too (ACE 4 265–267).

The executioners cannot remove the brown, seamless robe woven by Mary for Jesus without removing the crown of thorns. They tear the crown from Jesus' wounded, bleeding head, remove the robe, and thrust the crown back in place. Next, they yank off the underclothing which is cemented with blood to His body. Mary prays earnestly and is ready to step forward with her veil to cover Jesus, when a man runs forward with a strip of linen for which Jesus thanks him and winds it around

Himself as the man bravely declares, "Let the Man cover Himself." It is Jonadab, the nephew of Joseph, who has come rushing to Golgotha on an impulse (ACE 4 269–271).

Strange weather, darkness at mid–afternoon, and an earthquake precede and coincide with Jesus' statement, "Father, into Thy hands I commend My spirit!" The nun calls Mary the Queen of Martyrs as she beholds her precious Son so torn, disfigured, and mangled between two murderers. The nun sees the luminous soul of Jesus penetrate the earth surrounded by angels, including Gabriel. She sees masses of evil spirits driven by the angels into the Abyss. Meanwhile the High Priests in the temple are slaughtering the lambs. All goes on until the corpses of the raised dead appear in the temple. The red, blue, white, and yellow curtain tears in two at the entrance to the Holy of Holies. Nicodemus and Joseph of Arimathea leave the temple. Annas, the High Priest, Jesus' principal enemy, rushes about in terror. The alarmed but disciplined Caiaphas tries to calm Annas. The nun continues describing in great detail the havoc occurring at Jesus' death (ACE 4 300–307).

It is customary to break the bones to hurry the deaths of those being crucified. By prophecy Jesus is not to have broken bones, and He does not. The two others on their crosses do suffer that fate and expire. Cassius, later called Longinus—an officer known for poor eyesight—fulfills another prophecy. He draws out his telescoping lance full length, adds the tip, and rides his horse up to a point where he can plunge the lance upward into Jesus' right side so that the point opens a small wound on the left breast. As he withdraws the lance, a great stream of blood and water rush out, pouring over Cassius' upturned face and into a hollow in the rock below. Suddenly, Cassius can see clearly both physically and spiritually. He springs from the horse and kneels, praising God and confessing Jesus as his Lord. Mary and the others cry out and rush to the cross. Mary feels, too, the thrust of the lance, but soon all are dipping up the precious blood and water with cups and pouring the sacred fluid into flasks. Then, they use linen cloths to soak up what cannot be dipped. The soldiers present also fall on their knees and honor the crucified Jesus. The executioners depart due to Pilate's order that Jesus' body is to be left for Joseph of Arimathea to bury. They had already dragged the thieves' bodies away. Mary, John, and a number of remaining holy women witness this latest outrage and miracle. They leave to gather things for the burial and give Mary some rest before the body is removed from the cross and prepared for burial (ACE 4 315–317).

Joseph and Nicodemus and servants come to the cross with all the necessary equipment to remove Jesus from the cross and prepare the body for burial in the new tomb owned by Joseph. On the way, they stop to take the Blessed Virgin and about four other women with them. Some of the holy women are still at the cross. Cassius and other con-verted soldiers stand ready to help. Magdalen grieves with great emo-tion. The men remove the body with great care, and the nun describes the scene fully. Finally, the men wrap the body in linen from the waist to the knees and then place it on a sheet in His mother's outstretched arms. She focuses on the beloved face while Magdalen kneels with her face on His feet. All help however best they can bringing water, sponges, towels, ointments, and spices. Mary works to remove all the thorns. She washes the face and sponges the dried blood from the head and re-maining hair. Each of the numberless wounds is tenderly cleansed. She proceeds to the upper body while holy women kneel beside her, hold-ing ointment to anoint the wounds. She tenderly kisses the nail–pierced hands. At the completion of the anointing of the wounds, Mary wraps linen around the head. She closes the wounded eyes lovingly, then the open mouth, and weeping bitterly rests her face upon His. Both the Mother and Magdalen are reluctant to let the men take the body to complete the cleansing and embalming. They feel the loss in great force again. The men complete preparing the body, adding herbs and spices and binding the body in linens. When they finish, John takes Mary and the other women to the body.

Mary removes a fine linen scarf from around her neck, a gift from Claudia Procla, and places it under Jesus' head. The women apply more costly ointments, powders, and herbs. Magdalen pours precious balm into the side wound. Finally, the body is all wrapped so as to appear like a mummy. Then they lay the body on a very large sheet brought by Joseph and wrap it about the body in a special manner. While they kneel around the body, shedding many tears of farewell, a miracle oc-

SEEKING INFORMATION ON

holistic health, spirituality, dreams, intuition or ancient civilizations?
Call 1-800-723-1112, visit our Web site, or mail in this postage-paid card for a FREE catalog of books and membership information.

Name: _____

Address: _____

City: _____

State/Province: _____

Postal/Zip Code: _____ Country: _____

Association for Research and Enlightenment, Inc.
215 67th Street
Virginia Beach, VA 23451-2061

For faster service, call 1-800-723-1112.
www.edgarcayce.org

PBIN

curs. The entire form of Jesus' wounded body appears in red and brown colors on the cloth covering the body. It is as though He is showing gratitude for their grief and loving care by leaving His imprint on this outer covering. In their astonishment, they decide to remove the covering and, in so doing, are even more amazed to see the interior linens white as ever—only the outside cover carries the image. The nun then gives a little history of the winding-sheet and how she sees the sheet in various visions, including Turin and also a time when in order to settle a dispute, the sheet is thrown into a fire. Miraculously it rises above the flames and into the hands of Christians (ACE 4 326–339).

All follow the body of Jesus to the tomb. They enter the cave and express their love for Jesus. Mary comes in last and sits by the body and weeps. Then they all leave as the Sabbath begins.

Later in the evening, the Apostles and disciples gradually gather at the place of the Last Supper. Mary and her companions return from their mission to Mt. Calvary. They go to Mary's apartment for refreshment. Those in Bethany come to join the mourners. That night, Joseph leaves at a late hour with some of the disciples and some of the holy women. All head for their homes. Suddenly, an armed band seizes Joseph. Caiaphas has directed the kidnapping and intends that Joseph be imprisoned to die of starvation.

Caiaphas and Pilate meet and discuss Jesus' statement that He will rise again in three days. Caiaphas sends twelve temple guards with lanterns to the tomb area. Pilate wants nothing more to do with Caiaphas' plans but sends Cassius to spy on the guards and keep him informed of what he sees. Cassius is a changed man and, as he sits or stands at the entrance to the tomb, he receives much interior enlightenment and understanding of many mysteries (ACE 4 339–345).

Mary and the holy women remaining with her retire for some rest. At midnight they arise, fold up their beds, gather around Mary and the lamp, and conduct their usual nocturnal prayers. John and some of the disciples knock on the door of the women's hall. It is about three in the morning when the group prepares to go to the temple since by custom the temple opens about midnight after the eating of the Paschal lamb. Due to all the disturbances of nature and the crucifixion, the temple is nearly deserted except for servants and guards. All is in disarray, and the risen dead visiting the temple have defiled it. The sons of Simeon and nephews of Joseph of Arimathea, very upset over their uncle's arrest, greet the Blessed Virgin and her companions. Since they are in charge of caring for the temple, they guide the group all over the temple. The destruction is quite extensive, and no attempt has been made to clear it away. All around the rent curtain, the supporting beam and pillars are displaced. The Holy of Holies is open to view. Walls are cracked, floors sunken, and pillars askew. Mary, followed by the others, revisits all the sacred sites of Jesus' visits. She kneels, kisses the spot, and tearfully relates her memories associated with the area. The others also honor the areas. Mary points out the teacher's chair where the boy Jesus astonishes the priests with His wisdom. Mary sees the physical temple nearly destroyed due to the sins of the people and recalls Jesus' weeping and prophesying, "Destroy this Temple, and in three days I will build it up again." Mary observes Jesus' enemies destroy the temple of His body. She longs for the third day and the true revelation of Jesus' words (ACE 4 346–350).

When the Sabbath ends, John, Peter, and James the Greater gather with the holy women so that they mourn together and comfort one another. After the men leave, the holy women wrap themselves in their mourning mantles and go to their separate rooms to pray among the strewn ashes.

The nun sees an angel appear to Mary. The message he brings is that the Lord is near, and Mary is to go to the gate owned by Nicodemus. She joyfully wraps her mantle about her and hurries to the city wall where the gate opens to the garden of the tomb. Suddenly, Mary stops and longingly gazes at the top of the wall. She sees the souls of ancient Patriarchs and the holy soul of Jesus gloriously illuminated. He points toward Mary and turns to the Patriarchs exclaiming, "This is Mary, My Mother!" and appears to embrace her. Then Jesus disappears. Mary sinks to her knees and kisses the ground where Jesus stood. The stones retain the imprints of her knees and feet. Wonderfully consoled, she hurries back to the holy women and finds them preparing ointment and spices. With renewed spirit, she strengthens the faith of the holy women but says nothing of her experience. In the city, Magdalen, Mary Cleophas, Johanna Chusa, and Mary Salome buy herbs, ointment, nard water, and flowers in pots (including a lovely iris) while Mary is absent. The disciples also carry some of these items, to be placed on or around Jesus' body. They do not come to speak to the women.

The nun has a vision of Joseph in the prison cell. Light suddenly fills the cell, and Joseph hears his name called. The roof rises at one side to admit a shining figure floating down a strip of linen. The angel tells Joseph to grasp the linen and hold on as he climbs the wall by stepping on the projecting stones. The roof resettles as soon as Joseph is free. He runs along the wall until he can climb down and knock at the door where the disciples are gathered. Joseph tells his joyful audience of his experience, and they feed him and thank God. Joseph goes to Arimathea that night and stays until it is safe to return to Jerusalem.

Emmerich sees the holy sepulcher and describes the guards and Cassius maintaining his watch as the lanterns shed their light. The body of Jesus has dazzling light surrounding it—with one angel at the head and one at the foot. They remind the nun of the cherubim of the Ark of the Covenant minus wings. The whole tomb seems to her like the Ark in different times of its history. She sees the souls of Jesus and the Patriarchs floating through the tomb, and Jesus points out the wounds on the now unbound and transparent body, to the souls who weep compassionately.

The next vision mysteriously shows the two angels floating with the prone body through the trembling rock to the throne of God. Amidst surrounding choirs of ecstatic angels, Jesus presents His wounded body.

Meanwhile back at the tomb, the guards fall unconscious and upon regaining consciousness agree they have witnessed an earthquake. Cassius observes the scene and is fearful and unable to understand it.

The holy women complete preparing what they will take to the tomb early the next morning and are afraid Jesus' enemies may interfere. Mary reassures them and they retire.

Mary cannot sleep and goes out alone going first to the house of Caiaphas and then to the palace of Pilate. Then she travels about the entire way of the cross. She seems to be seeking something lost. She frequently kneels, feels the stones and now and then touches her lips to them. It is the drops of blood that appear as lights. She continues to Mount Calvary. She gazes at an apparition of Jesus. An angel precedes Him, and the two angels of the tomb are at His side. They seem to float in light. Jesus speaks to His mother of His experience in limbo. Next, He tells he is about to leave the tomb with a glorified body. She is to wait for Him at a certain stone. Mary kneels and prays. The Lord's procession proceeds over the way of the cross with the angels gathering any and all flesh and blood torn from Jesus' body. Mary sees all taking place in spirit. The body again rests in the tomb, and the angels miraculously replace all pieces that had been lost from the body. Jesus' soul floats down into the body. Then, the nun sees the body again containing the soul of Jesus in a dazzling light come from the side of the winding sheet. This reminds the nun of Eve coming out of Adam's side.

Immediately, in another Emmerich vision, a human-headed dragon coils up out of the abyss, lashing its tail and looking angrily at the Lord. The Redeemer has a white staff with a little standard on the top. He plants a foot on the dragon's head and strikes three blows of the staff on its tail. It shrinks and sinks into the earth with the face the last to disappear. At the moment of Jesus' conception, the nun sees a similar serpent, which looks like the tempting serpent of paradise. She believes these visions all refer to, "The seed of the woman shall crush the serpent's head." The whole scene to her is symbolical of victory over death. The tomb vanishes from her sight at the crushing of the serpent's head. The Lord floats up through the trembling rock; an angel rolls the stone away and sits on it. The lanterns swing from side to side, and the guards again fall unconscious. Cassius does not see the Lord, but he sees the angels and rushes to the stone couch feeling the empty linens. The nun sees the risen Lord appear to Mary on Mt. Calvary with His wounds sparkling. The Patriarchs bow low before the Blessed Mother. Jesus shows Mary His wounds and tells her He will see her again. She falls to her knees to kiss His feet. He takes her hand and raises her up, then disappears (ACE 4 359–367).

At this point, the story of the holy women arriving begins. The Bible describes it. How very fortunate that the holy nun gives us the rest of the story. How apt that Jesus appears to His sinless mother twice before He appears to any others. Of course, it is very comforting that He next appears to a woman from whom He cleans layers and layers of the prince of the world's temptations. Magdalen, filled with undying gratitude and pure spiritual love for her Savior, is a perfect example of the truly and wholly repentant sinner.

Eve receives the blame for ruining God's plan for the redemption of fallen man, but Adam fails to obey also and both suffer greatly. However, it seems that even today women, especially those in the same part of the world where Jesus and Mary lived, are still suffering to an even greater extent than men. Jesus and Mary exemplify forgiveness. The holy women do not desert them, and Jesus and Mary greatly respect these faithful women and elevate the place of women considerably. The prince of this world prefers revenge to forgiveness and successfully contributes to the degradation of women.

Nicodemus prepares a love feast for the Apostles, the holy women, and the disciples in the entrance hall next to the room of the Last Supper. The holy women sit at the same table with the men. There is much instruction by Peter and John. A feeling of oneness pervades these groups. They declare they will have all things in common and live perfectly united. The nun sees light flooding the room and the people appearing to dissolve into one another. "All seemed to resolve into a pyramid of light in which the Blessed Virgin appeared to be not only the apex but the radiant center of all. All graces flow in streams from Mary down upon the Apostles, and from them back again through her to the Lord (ACE 4 376–378).

Mary liked to be in Jerusalem as she could go at twilight and walk the way of the cross, praying and meditating where Jesus suffered a fall. However, because some of these spots are now hedged in or filled up, she simply duplicates the pathway at her home as she knows it by heart. She originates this practice and continues it the rest of her life (ACE 4 393).

When Jesus appears to the Apostles, with Thomas present and seeing Jesus for the first time since the Resurrection, Jesus explains that He is commissioning Peter to confirm his brothers. For this ceremony, John brings on his arm a large, brightly embroidered mantle made by Mary and the holy women. It is white with red stripes and certain symbols. Wheat, grapes, and a lamb appear embroidered in different colors. It is wide and long and has a collar with a blue hood. Peter kneels before Jesus who gives him a shining morsel, and then Jesus breathes on Peter in a special way. He also puts His mouth to Peter's mouth and then to his ears. Jesus also lays His hands on Peter, and all these actions give Peter strength of a special kind. Next, Jesus places the mantle made by the holy women on Peter, telling him it will preserve the strength just imparted to him. Peter then gives a very moving address. Jesus vanishes while Peter is speaking (ACE 4 397).

During another appearance of the risen Jesus, the nun sees Him explaining how much Adam and Eve lost due to their fall and how happy they now are that His sacrifice frees them from the effects of the fall. Emmerich again shows that man's creation is for the purpose of filling up the places of the angelic choirs fallen from heaven. Adam and Eve needed to obey God, so that man will multiply to the required number to fill the incomplete choirs. Then creation will end. But the fall causes great changes and a mixing of purity and darkness. Death becomes necessary and a kindness to man. The nun feels the end of the world will not occur "until all the wheat is separated from the chaff and those choirs of the fallen angels filled up with it" (ACE 4 405–406).

Jesus appears to the five hundred and gives the Sermon on the Mount. The Apostles, many disciples, and all the holy women including Mary are present. Peter and five Apostles teach the people before Jesus appears. The holy women stand near one of the paths, and, when Jesus arrives on that path, they prostrate before Him, and He speaks to them. Jesus speaks very plainly to the crowd, describing what will be the cost of following Him, including abandoning relatives and enduring persecution. About two hundred listeners leave after that description. To the Apostles and disciple, He gives some specific instructions. This is Jesus' principal appearance in Galilee after His resurrection. It is also His most public appearance as the others are more secret.

A gathering of nearly three hundred of the faithful, including fifty women, takes place in Bethany. Most of these women in attendance give all of their belongings to the Community. This gathering includes a love-feast of breaking bread and passing the cup in Lazarus's court. Peter gives an instruction before a great crowd in which spies stand and make derisive remarks. Peter is a changed man since the ceremony Jesus conducts, when Peter receives the mantle made by the holy women and the special powers given by Jesus.

About fifty temple guards from Jerusalem appear in Bethany. Deputies interrogate the Apostles, but the magistrates in Bethany oppose the deputies and tell them to state charges if they have any but to stop disturbing the peace. Peter dismisses the group to avoid offending temple guards, but he tells all to return for Christ's ascension. The fifty women already live in groups so that they just return to their places.

In Jerusalem the Jews clear from offices any who favor Jesus or the disciples. In an attempt to destroy anything honored by those faithful to Jesus, some streets become dead ends to prevent anyone from following the way of the cross. Hedges, pit falls, and beams cause Mount Calvary to be impassable. Because Nicodemus owns the property on which the tomb lies, it is not desecrated (ACE 4 407–412).

The next day after the disruption in Bethany, the Apostles, about twenty disciples, the Blessed Virgin, all the holy women, Joseph, Nicodemus, Lazarus, and Obed gather in the house of the Last Supper. Peter and John speak to the disciples and Apostles to inform them of a communication from Jesus, regarding their relationship with Mary. Emmerich sees the Blessed Virgin in spirit hovering over the two groups. Her shining mantle spreads out to embrace all, and a crown descends from the Holy Trinity through the heaven above her to sit on her head. This is in contrast to the usual position of Mary kneeling in prayer outside the hall. The nun interprets this scene as symbolizing that Mary is head of all of them, and the temple inclosing all.

A little later, a meal is served in the outer hall. The guests are in special robes, and Mary, sitting between Peter and John at the Apostles table, is wearing her wedding gown. At the end of the meal, they break bread and drink wine, but it is not consecrated. Near midnight the nun sees the Blessed Virgin and the Apostles in the supper room. She stands between Peter and John under the prayer lamp. They kneel before the

Holy of Holies and pray. At midnight the Virgin kneels and receives the Blessed Sacrament (previously consecrated by Jesus) from Peter. Jesus appears only to her while she is in prayer and penetrated with light. The Apostles treat her very reverently as she goes to her nearby apartment. Once inside, she stands and recites the Magnificat, the Canticle of the three youths in the fiery furnace, and the 130th Psalm. Jesus later enters through closed doors and speaks at length with Mary. He explains how she is to help the Apostles and what she is to be to them. He gives her power over the whole Church. In a manner the nun finds hard to express, Jesus imparts His strength and protection to Mary. It is transported through a penetrating light. A crown of stars encircles her head as it did at her communion. Another mysterious concept revealed to the nun has to do with communion. The Blessed Virgin's communion bread would always remain unchanged in her body so that she would always have the sacramental presence of the God–man preserved in her holy heart living tabernacle. Mary alone has this special grace (ACE 4 413–415).

The house of the Last Supper becomes the temple for the followers of Jesus. This is a fairly large complex. The holy of holies is in the Last Supper room. The various halls and courts provide much space for crowds to gather. Both Mary and John have apartments in another area. A great many newcomers from other lands and other areas of the holy land come to Jerusalem and Bethany. Lazarus helps greatly in providing space. Actually, Peter's wife and daughter, Mark's wife, and other women coming from Bethsaida to Bethany dwell in tents as previously stated. Many of the women, including Mary, work with weaving, making tent covers, and embroidering special vestments and robes. Although much help is given to find space for the tents or rooms and apartments, they are not at once admitted to the Community, nor do they have access to the house of the Last Supper. Neither the new arrivals nor the Apostles and disciples frequent the Jewish temple. The Apostles go there after Pentecost to preach to the multitudes. Mary, the Blessed Virgin is considered the mother of all. The Apostles consult her and consider her an exceptional Apostle among the group (ACE 4 417).

Jesus appears quite naturally to the Apostles, talking and eating with them. Some who oppose Jesus see him at times, too, and are terrified. He continues to spread blessings wherever He goes, and many, after seeing him, join the disciples. On the last day before His Ascension, many of the faithful gather in Bethany because they know Jesus is soon to leave. They want this last opportunity to see Him. Mary and many other holy women come, too. When Jesus arrives at Lazarus' house, many of the disciples start weeping. Jesus does not want them weeping and points out to them that His mother, standing with the holy women, is *not* weeping (ACE 4 420).

The night before the Ascension, Jesus is in the house of the Last Supper's inner hall with the Apostles and the Blessed Virgin. The disciples and holy women are praying in the side halls. The communion table stands in the supper room with the Paschal bread and chalice on it. Mary stands opposite Jesus. The Apostles are in their ceremonial robes. The nun sees the consecrated bread enter the Apostles' mouths in a luminous form. Jesus' words consecrating the wine flow into the chalice like streaming red light. Magdalen, Martha, and Mary Cleophas during this last day also receive the sacraments (ACE 4 423-424).

Before leaving the house the next morning, Jesus presents the Blessed Virgin to those gathered as their Mother, Mediatrix, and Advocate. Mary then bestows upon Peter and all the rest her blessing. All bow low to Mary. Emmerich at that moment sees Mary on a throne with a light blue mantle about her and a crown on her head to signify she is the Queen of Mercy.

Jesus leaves the house in Jerusalem at dawn with the Apostles and the Blessed Virgin following. The disciples follow at a little distance. They are taking the route of the Palm Sunday procession. Jesus leads them over the path of His Passion. When there are obstructions, Jesus sends the disciples ahead to clear them. Just before turning toward Mount Calvary, they stop under shade trees. Jesus teaches and comforts. Many others join the procession, but the nun sees no women in the group.

The same people in Jerusalem present for the Palm Sunday procession appear now, making a great crowd of people. The Lord goes to Gethsemane and, from the Garden of Olives, He walks to the mountain's summit. By the time He reaches the top, He appears as a beam of white sunlight. A circle of rainbow light falls around Him. Putting His left hand on His chest, He turns slowly while raising His right hand, blessing the whole world. He appears to be absorbed into the light from above, joining with the light coming from Himself. The nun sees many souls joining in that light and vanishing with the Lord in a cloud of light. Then a dew or shower of light seems to fall lightly on those below. The men appear amazed, but The Blessed Virgin gazes calmly ahead (ACE 4 424–427).

At first the Apostles and disciples feel lonely, restless, and forsaken, but Mary's soothing presence comforts them. They take to heart Jesus' words as to her being to them a mediatrix, a mother, and an advocate and feel at peace. For the next several days they stay together in the house of the last supper. Mary sits opposite Peter in the prayer–circle and at meals takes Jesus' position. Mathias, rather than Joses Barsabas becomes the twelfth Apostle (ACE 4 428–429).

The time of Pentecost arrives. The room of the Last Supper is ornamented for the occasion. Peter wears his Episcopal robe. The Blessed Virgin with veiled face stands in the entrance hall with the holy women. Peter breaks and distributes the bread he has blessed—first to Mary and then to the Apostles and disciples. All, including Mary, kiss his hand upon receiving the bread.

Toward morning of the next day, a glittering white cloud appears above the Mount of Olives and draws near the house of the Last Supper. Many see the cloud and tremble. The luminous cloud descends low over the house, the sound and light intensifying. The Apostles, disciples, and women become silent. Streams of white light shoot from the cloud with a rushing wind. The gathered faithful become ecstatic, and their heads throw back involuntarily with their mouths open. Into each mouth flows a fire–like tongue of light. It seems as though they are eagerly drinking in the fire. It pours forth on the Apostles, disciples, and the women. The tongues of fire are different colors. The emotional people all gather around the calm, quiet, Blessed Virgin. All seem infused with new life, and they embrace one another and then give prayers of thanks and praise. Peter gives some instruction and then sends several to the inns housing Pentecost guests. He places his hands on the five Apostles who are to assist in the teaching and baptizing. Before they leave for the Pool of Bethsaida to consecrate the water and baptize, they kneel to receive the benediction of the Blessed Virgin. She gives this blessing whenever the Apostles leave and return. For these ceremonies, she wears a white mantle, an off-white veil, and a sky-blue embroidered scarf that hangs to the ground on either side. It is held in place by a white silk crown. Peter stands in the teacher's chair to speak to the crowd before the baptisms begin. He and other Apostles instruct the people, and all are amazed that they hear the words in their own language.

The baptismal service begins after Peter, John, and James the Less solemnly bless the water. They add more water from a flask of water blessed by Jesus. Mary and the holy women help by distributing baptismal garments to the neophytes. The baptismal candidate leans over the railing. Then an Apostle scoops up water in a basin and pours water three times over the head. The holy women not already baptized this day receive baptism. About three thousand people join the Community that day. The preaching and baptizing continue on the following day (ACE 4 430–435).

The old synagogue at the Pool of Bethsaida is taken over by the followers of Jesus, who work hard to repair it and make it into a church. The nun gives a lengthy description of it and the pool where the baptisms occur (ACE 4 437). The Last Supper room continues to be used by the Apostles for such ceremonies as the one in which six disciples are advanced to the rank of priests. The Sacraments remain here and are presented in a certain order. Peter receives the bread and wine first. Then he serves John and James the Less. John then hands the Sacrament first to Mary and then to the Apostles and the six disciples who are being ordained priests. Mary brings the vestments for the new priests and lays them on the altar. The six ordained are Eliud, son of the aged Simeon, Nathanael, Zacheus, Barnabas, John Mark, and Joses Barsabas. The mothers of the last two are the holy women Mary Marcus and Mary Cleophas (ACE 4 442–443).

Peter, John, several of the disciples, Mary and other holy women go to the temple one afternoon. A lame man lies at the door of the temple, and Peter and John speak with him. Then Peter makes a heated speech to people gathered there. Some priests and soldiers confer. The lame man asks Peter for alms after his speech. Peter gives the famous reply about having no silver or gold, but says he will give what he has. With John's help, he heals the man. The man leaps about, and a crowd gathers. Peter goes into the forecourt and starts teaching from the teacher's chair where Jesus taught at twelve. The temple soldiers seize Peter, John, and the cured man and throw them in a prison near the judgment hall where Peter previously denied the Lord. The other Apostles pray all night long in the Last Supper house for the prisoners' release. The next day they stand before Caiaphas and other priests. Peter speaks vigorously, and they are set free. James the Less reveals to them that Jesus foresees the occurrence of this set of circumstances and that afterwards they are all to retire for awhile from the area (ACE 4 447).

The Apostles shut up everything, and Peter carries the Blessed Sacrament around his neck in a bag. They go to Bethany in three groups. Mary and the other women go, too. The Apostles preach enthusiastically but finally return to Jerusalem. Peter teaches to the people in the church at the pool and tells them now is the time to labor, to suffer persecution, and give up all belongings. He invites those not prepared to do that to leave. About one hundred recent converts leave (ACE 4 448–449).

Stephen is stoned to death about a year after Jesus' crucifixion, but persecution of the Apostles does not increase. However, converts stop settling around Jerusalem, Christians disperse, and some are murdered. A few years later prejudice against them greatly increases. John and Mary decide she should move near Ephesus as many Christians have settled there. At this time Lazarus, Martha, and Magdalen set out over the sea after being imprisoned and released. Mary moves. John returns to Jerusalem to be with the other Apostles. James tries to go to Spain, but spies attempt to keep him from leaving Palestine. Friends in Joppa get him underway. He sails to Ephesus to visit Mary and then goes to Spain. He visits Mary and John a second time, and Mary tells him he will soon meet his death in Jerusalem. As Emmerich sees that James is arrested and led toward Mount Calvary, she notices that all sites associated with Jesus are eliminated. James keeps preaching and cures a lame man. Then Josias, who denounced James, comes up to ask James for forgiveness and declares he is for Christ. James embraces him and kisses him telling him he will be baptized in his own blood. Because of Josias' declaring for Christ, he, too, receives a death sentence. They bind James to a large stone and behead him. This occurs about twelve years after Jesus' death (ACE 4 449–451).

Before Mary moves near Ephesus, John builds a stone house for her similar to her house in Nazareth. It has two apartments, and with the use of screens, room can be divided. Mary's maid servant lives with her, and occasionally holy women (some her relatives) come to visit. Mary has an oratory containing a Crucifix made by the Blessed Virgin and John (ACE 4 452–453).

Mary leads a very quiet life near Ephesus and longs to be freed from earth. She is at least a quarter of an hour from any of the other Christian settlers and neighbors. Her maid obtains what she needs. Sometimes, a traveling Apostle visits Mary. John is not a frequent visitor. During one visit, the nun reports that John looks thin and much older. The maid conducts Mary to John. She is in a white robe and is quite weak. Her face is white as snow. John and Mary kneel and pray before the Crucifix a long time. John arises and takes from a metal box a small piece of white bread rolled in fine wool. With a few words, he serves this Blessed Sacrament to Mary (ACE 4 454–456).

Near her stone house, Mary herself constructs the twelve Stations of the Cross as soon as possible after her move. She knows the number of steps between the stations by heart and starts with that information. Walking the right number of steps, she places memorial stones and so on until the path is laid out. She and her maid walk the holy way silently and pray at each station. Gradually, the way is improved. John has regular memorials made of marble and then placed. The cave that serves as the Sepulcher is cleared and prepared for a place to pray. The nun believes Mary's remains actually rested in that tomb. Mary has a special costume she wears when she walks the Way of the Cross. It is the one she wears at the crucifixion under her mantle. On one occasion, the nun sees Mary and five other women walking the way, but she does not specifically name them. She does refer to them as holy women (ACE 4 456–458).

Three years after Mary's move to near Ephesus, she has a strong desire to visit Jerusalem. John and Peter take her there. Several Apostles including Thomas are in a Council, and Mary offers her advice. In the evening, Peter and John escort her to all the places Mary considers holy and desires to visit. She becomes so moved by compassion that they must support her.

Less than two years before her death, she travels once more from Ephesus to Jerusalem and visits the holy places. She murmurs for her Son and becomes very sorrowful. Her companions fear she is going to die and consider preparing a tomb. Mary suggests a cave on Mount Olivet, and the Apostles have a Christian stone cutter build a beautiful tomb. The nun claims that John Damascene writes from hearsay that Mary died in Jerusalem and is buried there. She believes the confusion occurs on purpose because of pagan sentiment of the time that might have caused Mary to be adored as a goddess (ACE 4 459).

Evidently Mary returns to Ephesus. Emmerich reports in detail the arrival of many to her death bed. She wants to fulfill her Son's directions. As she feels the end coming, she calls the Apostles to her by prayer. She wants to bless them and say to them the words Jesus instructed her to say. Therefore, through angels the Apostles receive the call to Ephesus. Peter is in Antioch, and Andrew is not far from there. One night an angel takes Peter by the hand and tells him to hasten to Mary. The angel says he will soon meet up with Andrew and continue with him. Peter is stiff from age and fatigue but dresses, and taking his staff starts off. He soon catches up with Andrew, and shortly they meet Jude Thaddeus. When they arrive at Mary's, they find John already there. Thomas receives the call in India. He is on his way to Tartary and wants to go there first. He receives a second summons and hurries to Ephesus. He does not return to Tartary as he is pierced by a sword in India. John starts from Jericho, and Bartholomew is in Asia east of the Red Sea. Paul is not summoned as only those related to or acquainted with the holy family receive the call.

Mary lies on her couch, being cared for by her sorrowful maid. Two of Mary's sisters and five disciples arrive looking exhausted. They all embrace and some weep to meet on this sad occasion. They sleep outside under light awnings, held up with posts and enclosed by screens. The first arrivals prepare a place for prayer and communion. Peter carries a cross from which he takes the sacraments and administers them to Mary while the Apostles bow low around the couch. The screens separating the front and back of the house are moved so that disciples and holy women can stand in the front apartment and yet see.

Mary sits upright in her bed, and the Apostles kneel in turn by her couch. She prays over each and blesses each with her hands laid upon the Apostle crosswise. She does the same with the disciples and holy women. One of the holy women bends low over Mary, and Mary embraces her. Peter has a roll of Scripture in his hand as he steps up to the couch. Mary speaks to all and tells them that Jesus in Bethany instructed her what to do and say in this situation. She tells John what to do with her remains and to divide her clothes between her maid and a woman of the neighborhood who often helps her. Peter conducts the Holy Mass in front of Mary's crucifix and serves the holy sacrament to all present. During this service Philip arrives from Egypt. He receives the blessing from Mary and then the sacraments from Peter.

John carries in a shallow dish the chalice containing Jesus' blood. Thaddeus brings a little incense–basin forward. Peter gives Mary the last anointing and then communion. She sinks back on the pillow. The Apostles pray briefly, and she receives the chalice from John. Mary speaks no more. A smile crosses her face as she departs. The roof seems to disappear leaving the lamp hanging in space. A pathway of light stretches from Mary up to the heavens. Angel faces peer out of the clouds of light on either side of the pathway. Mary raises her arms to heaven. Her body floats so high above the couch that light appears between body and couch. A figure of light issues from Mary's body. Choirs of angels take up the figure and soar with it as the body sinks back to the couch, the hands crossed over the breast. The nun sees many holy souls coming to meet Mary: Joseph, Anna, Joachim, John the Baptist, Zachary and Elizabeth. They follow her as she soars on up to her Son whose wounds are shining brilliant flashing light. He places in her hand a scepter while pointing at the whole earth. Next, the nun sees a great many souls released from purgatory following Mary to heaven.

Peter and John have their faces turned upward so that they probably see the glorious rising of Mary's soul. The other Apostles are kneeling with bowed heads. Mary's body lies radiant with light. All kneel and praise God.

Finally, the women cover the blessed remains with a sheet, push all the furniture aside and cover it and the fireplace. All present cover their heads—veils for the women and scarves for the men—and take turns praying two at a time, one at the head and the other at the foot of the remains. They also go to walk the Way of the Cross. Andrew sets up a door in front of the tomb, and the women prepare the body for burial. Veronica's daughter and John Mark's mother are two of the women.

The whole house becomes like a little chapel with someone always praying. The body is lifted in the bed linen into a long basket with a cover. The women cut a few locks of hair as relics. They place herbs all about the body.

John carries a vessel of oil, and Peter anoints the forehead, hands, and feet of the holy body with the form of the cross while praying. The body is then enveloped in linens by the women. The covered coffin of snow-white wood is covered with an arched lid and fastened with straps, then placed on a litter. The Apostles take turns carrying the coffin, and the rest follow the coffin. At the grotto, four of the Apostles carry the coffin in and place it in the hollow of the tomb. All go in one by one to kneel in prayer and take leave of the body.

They shut the tomb and make a trench before the entrance to the grotto, planting it quite thickly with flowers and berry bushes so that it can be entered only from the side with difficulty.

The night following the burial, the bodily assumption of the Blessed Virgin occurs. Several of the Apostles and holy women are in the garden praying and singing Psalms by the grotto. The nun sees a broad pathway of light descending from heaven to the tomb. Groups of angels surround the resplendent soul of the Blessed Virgin which comes floating down. Her Divine Son accompanies her, his wounds flashing. The various circles of light contain angels from very young appearing ones in the innermost circle to youthful appearing ones in the outer circle. Some of the people present gaze upward in amazement and adoration, while others are prostrate and fearful on the earth.

The soul of Mary penetrates into the tomb and rises again radiant with light in her glorified body, which is escorted to heaven by the Christ and the angels (ACE 4 460–470).

The next day Thomas and two companions arrive. Thomas grieves greatly when he learns the Blessed Virgin is already buried. He throws himself on the spot where she died and weeps. Finally the Apostles, who are singing in chorus when Thomas and his companions arrive, now come to embrace them and give them some food. Then they take them to the tomb and make it possible for them to enter the tomb. John loosens the straps and removes the lid. The winding-sheets are empty as shells and perfectly ordered. After all have come to look, they remove all the linens to keep as relics and return to the house by the Way of the Cross as they sing.

The Apostles and disciples stand together and relate their experiences. They tell where they have been serving their missions. Then, before they leave the little house, they raise an embankment before the tomb so that it is completely inaccessible. In the back wall of the tomb they create an opening where one who knows of the action can look into the tomb. They make a little church of the house but leave the front apartment for Mary's maid. They beautify the garden. Peter leaves two of the disciples there to accommodate the faithful in that area. The Apostles embrace and take leave of each other and the holy women after one more solemn service in Mary's house.

It is thirteen years and two months after Christ's Ascension when Mary dies. She is in her sixty-third year and ready to be reunited with her Holy Son and their heavenly Father. God surely must have greeted this most holy woman with, "Well done, thou good and faithful daughter" (ACE 4, 451, 460, 471–473).

A.R.E. PRESS

The A.R.E. Press publishes books, videos, and audiotapes meant to improve the quality of our readers' lives—personally, professionally, and spiritually. We hope our products support your endeavors to realize your career potential, to enhance your relationships, to improve your health, and to encourage you to make the changes necessary to live a loving, joyful, and fulfilling life.

For more information or to receive a free catalog, call:

1–800–723–1112

Or write:

A.R.E. Press
215 67th Street
Virginia Beach, VA 23451-2061

DISCOVER HOW THE EDGAR CAYCE MATERIAL CAN HELP YOU!

The Association for Research and Enlightenment, Inc. (A.R.E.®), was founded in 1931 by Edgar Cayce. Its international headquarters are in Virginia Beach, Virginia, where thousands of visitors come year-round. Many more are helped and inspired by A.R.E.'s local activities in their own hometowns or by contact via mail (and now the Internet!) with A.R.E. headquarters.

People from all walks of life, all around the world, have discovered meaningful and life-transforming insights in the A.R.E. programs and materials, which focus on such areas as personal spirituality, holistic health, dreams, family life, finding your best vocation, reincarnation, ESP, meditation, and soul growth in small-group settings. Call us today at our toll-free number:

1-800-333-4499

or

Explore our electronic visitors center on the
Internet: **http://www.edgarcayce.org.**

We'll be happy to tell you more about how the work of the A.R.E. can help you!

A.R.E.
215 67th Street
Virginia Beach, VA 23451-2061